Memory Lane

ELY
AND THE FENS

Memory Lane
ELY
AND THE FENS

Mike Petty MBE

Cambridge News

First published in Great Britain in 2001 by The Breedon Books Publishing Company Limited, Breedon House, 3 The Parker Centre, Derby, DE21 4SZ.

Paperback reprint published in Great Britain in 2011 by The Derby Books Publishing Company Limited, 3 The Parker Centre, Derby, DE21 4SZ.

ISBN 978-1-85983-957-7

Printed and bound by Melita Press, Malta

Contents

Introduction

THE Cathedral City of Ely dominates the countryside north of Cambridge, standing high above the surrounding fenland as it has done for many centuries. While the Cathedral seems unchanging, thanks to an unprecedented period of restoration and renovation, innovation and adaptation, the area around it has been undergoing considerable changes within the last 40 years. Much which was yesterday an everyday part of the scene has now become just a memory. The RAF Hospital, Ely High School, the Rex Cinema, the Sugar Beet Factory, the Grunty Fen Express, the Mepal Nuclear Missile Base... all gone

The redevelopment of the Ely Market Place in the 1960s heralded what was hoped to be a major improvement in the shopping facilities of the city, replacing the Public Room and the Corn Exchange where farmers and dealers would gather from around the region. Just across the road was the Cattle Market, now replaced by another new shopping development, the Cloisters, which itself superseded a previous new shopping facility, Club Mews. A Tesco supermarket opened in October 1965 but proposals in 1975 for a new Keymarket supermarket in Angel Drove met with opposition from planners and other traders who feared it would draw trade away from the centre. The scheme was rejected. Soon, however, Tesco was expanding, with a new store replacing the Crin-o-lite lampshade factory in Broad Street opening in 1982 and yet another in 1994, down on the site opposed 20 years before.

These changes, together with the businesses that have gone – the White Hart, Post Office, Theobalds, Rickwoods and the rest are reflected here. Shops need customers, customers need to get to the shops. The growth of cars and the problems associated with them form part of the story, from the building of a new Board Street car park in 1965 to the banning of cars from the High Street on Market Day in 2000.

Villages too have seen the loss of their shopping facilities, their pubs, schools and blacksmiths. They have gained 'best-kept village' awards and bypasses but lost their 'characters' – some of whom are to be found among these pages.

These changes have been reported in the columns of the *Cambridge Evening News* and captured in pictures by its photographers. They have compiled the most comprehensive pictorial record anywhere of life in post-war Ely and area in all its complexity.

I have tried where possible to locate the actual captions that accompanied the pictures when they were first published. The opinions are thus those of the time, expressing the hopes and fears of the period. Sometimes events will have turned out better than people feared, at other times they are worse than they hoped.

Inevitably there will be things that have been forgotten that you would wish to have had remembered, pictures taken over the years which have not made their way into the *News* library files, more memories than can be crammed into the current book.

Please continue to share them through the pages of the *Cambridge Evening News* for as this selection makes clear, today has a habit of becoming history very quickly!

Mike Petty,
Stretham,
Ely
Summer 2001

Ely City

Looking down on St Mary's church in the November sunshine, 1991. (*News*, 14 November 1991. neg C7395.91.21)

Youngsters make the most of the deep snow by using up their energy in a snowball fight in St Mary's Street, 1968. (neg 10020/P/7)

The Old Fire Engine House Restaurant has become one of Ely's principal attractions – as the *News* reported in August 1968 soon after its opening: *Sculpture, tea, walled garden, wines … the attractions of the Old Fire Engine House at Ely are mixed on the menu in a charmingly casual way. "But then everything is done on rather a casual basis", said the manageress, Miss Ann Ford, "and all the staff here turn their hands to various jobs." Opened in June to serve cold lunches, morning coffee and afternoon tea, the restaurant is run largely by amateurs, except for the cook, Mrs Judi Fulford, who has a Cordon Bleu Certificate. The manageress makes salads, the secretary, Mrs Debbie Prince-White, takes a turn at waitressing when the demand for afternoon teas reaches a peak, and the waitress, a student, Suzanne*

Dhenin, gives a hand with the dishes, while the washer-up, a 16-year-old schoolboy, Bob Baxter, who has a flair for baking, mixes up sponges in the lulls between the dish-washing. And on the first Sunday the café opened – to an unexpected 130 afternoon teas – weekend guests of the staff were pressed into service too.

In this picture, staff at the Old Fire Engine House are (from the left) Debbie Prince-White (secretary), Judi Fulford (cook), Raine Stevens (part owner), Ann Ford (manageress) and Suzanne Dhenin (waitress) (*News*, 9 August 1968. neg 7217/P/28)

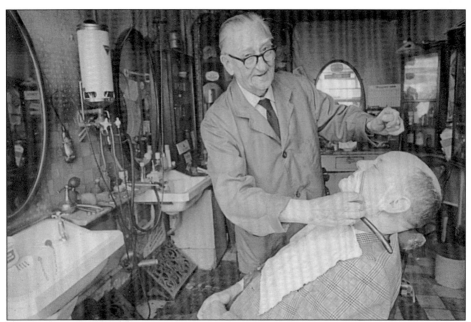

Nearby, the *News* reported in September 1974, Ely estate agent John Grain was enjoying a shave at the hands of an Ely hairdresser, *Mr Fred Dobson is still shaving customers and tending hair at the age of 83. The family business started in 1739 and now, five generations later, is entering its last chapter. Mr Dobson is famous for the bald patches recipe cure perfected through the five generations of the business. He was also well-known for his wigs. In Mr Dobson's museum-cum-salon in St Mary's Street hangs a reproduction of a 1730s print displaying his great, great, great grandfather shaving a jolly, sideboarded customer.* (*News*, 13 September 1974. neg 2463/74/13a)

One topic of conversation in the barber's chair has been Ely's commercial success: an elevated view along the High Street for the Christmas Shopping supplement in November 1965. (*News*, 26 November 1965. neg 6702/C)

The *News* commented: *Colourful and well-designed window displays, a repeat of the popular and much-admired decorative street lighting, with a star in the centre of each span, and as an innovation the introduction of a dozen eight-foot high 'Mod' angels erected at strategic points. These are amongst the attractions, which allied to top class salesmanship, excellent service and ingenuity, are certain to make yet another Ely and district chamber of trade 'shopping week' a success. It will spotlight the ability of trading establishments to supply, in wide variety and quality, all the shopping public's needs. The street illuminations have in past years bought praise from a wide area and set a pattern followed by other towns. The 'Mod' angels complete with golden crowns and candlesticks are illuminated at the head and feet and placed in positions where it would be difficult to extend the decorative lights. The chamber's president W.A.T. Rayment said "I believe there are definite advantages to shopping in Ely, and for the customers coming in from the villages by car. Parking facilities are reasonable and we now have an additional car park adjacent to the shopping area at the rear of Fore Hill.* (News, 29 November 1965. neg 6701/C)

High Street in June 1968 showing Lipton's supermarket. Later it was occupied by a Presto supermarket which closed suddenly in September 1987 and reopened as a new-style Argos catalogue showroom. (*News,* June 1968. neg 7216/P/29)

Ely's expanding range of shops, which include one of the country's leading fashion stores and a wide variety of other shops where residents and visitors can do their shopping, are becoming increasingly busy as Christmas approaches. (*News*, 8 December 1977. neg 2173.77.13)

Shoppers outside Boots the Chemist in March 1980; the shop moved to larger premises in Market Street. (*News*, 7 March 1980. neg 80780)

Several peoples' favourite shops have stopped trading, as the *News* reported in April 1982: *An Ely drapery shop is to close – forced out of business by an enormous increase in rent. S.J. Theobald and Co. has been trading at 23 High Street for about 24 years. Mr Theobald said a 16-fold increase in rent for the shop had been the main reason for the decision to close. "Such an enormous increase has made it uneconomic to continue with the trade we have", he said. The other reason was the very high staff cost. The shop was divided into five separate rooms, all of which had to be staffed.*

"Added to that, trade in Ely has suffered greatly since the shut down of such places as the sugar beet factory", he said. (News, 20 April 1982. neg 1399.82.29)

Various schemes have been produced to reduce traffic congestion and make shopping easier. This report appeared in November 1968: *A suggestion by the Surveyor, that the west side of Market Place should be closed to traffic on Thursday market days has been greeted by a storm of protest from traders. Mr Stroud said it would be of advantage to the public if the road were closed to traffic on Thursdays between 9am and 6 pm. "This would enable pedestrians to walk from the market to the central core of the town without crossing the traffic stream. Market stalls could be resited in the roadway, leaving the widest paved area opposite the Post Office free for seats, pictorial maps etc." Traders who were to be affected described it as ridiculous, pointless and impossible. Mr Francis Kempton, fruiterer said: "We have people making regular deliveries every day. If they can't park outside in the road they won't park anywhere. There are enough restrictions in this town anyway and the council are just chasing trade away." Bowgen's, the bakers, would certainly come to a standstill because they relied on seven van deliveries a day from the bakery, said the manageress, Mrs Jo Brown. Next door Mr Percy Newstead, the fishmonger, said a closure was likely to cause a loss of trade because people would not be able to park outside the shop. The manager of Green and White, the off-licence, Mr E.G. Chapman said: "This is impossible. I have two drays and about 10 other deliveries on Thursdays. I shall fight this and I shall have some of the big companies behind me. Shops in the partly-empty Market Place block, whose communal service area has its only access from the road on the west side of the Market Place would also be affected. A spokesman for Radio Relay, the television rental firm said access to the front of their shop was already closed to traffic on Thursdays because of the market. Now it looked as if the service area might be cut off as well. "If the road is closed the vans will become immobile if they are left in the yard. The whole idea of the run-in at the back is to get the vans off the road. And if we leave the vans outside then we will have to carry the television sets all over town to get to them", he said. (News, 6 November 1968. neg 1196/R)*

The pedestrian-only Buttermarket is a mixture of old and 1960s developments: *As well as old buildings, Ely has modern shopping centres, like this little square near the Market Place.* (*News*, 12 December 1979. neg 3415.79.18)

Thursday is market day, but when the fair arrived on the Market Place stall-holders had to move their stalls alongside the walls of the Cathedral precincts. The stalls have probably been moved like this since medieval times when the fair started. (*News*, 25 February 1978. neg 2397/21a). In 2000 the Council decided to close High Street to traffic on Saturdays and Thursday Market Day and planned to allow more market stalls along the street. In 2001, the Thursday ban was relaxed following opposition from many shopkeepers that echoed many of the points made in 1968.

In October 1978 the Mayor of Ely, Coun Henry Constable opened the City's October fair and then the Mayor and his wife Mabel rode on the speedway and dodgems. Accompanied by other members of the city council and the Chairman of East Cambridgeshire District Council, Mr Jeremy Newport, he then visited side stalls, stopping to try his hand at darts. (*News*, 27 October 1978. neg 3071.78.22) The fair has now been moved from the Market Place.

Plans for the transformation of the Market Place were prepared in the early 1960s. The Public Room which had served as a cinema since May 1919 closed in May 1963 in preparation for a new shopping centre. (*News*, 13 May 1963)

The Victorian Corn Exchange, erected in 1847 was used as a corn market for the last time in December 1962: *A tradition which has existed for 115 years passed quietly into history at Ely when the Corn Exchange was used for the last time as a corn market, the purpose for which it was built in 1847. Recently purchased by a London development company, it is scheduled to be replaced by a modern shopping centre.*

Only a handful of farmers, corn merchants and representatives of seed, feeding stuffs, fertilisers, oil and seed companies turned up for the building's last two-hour use as an indoor market. Before the war as many as 300 people from all parts of the eastern counties and from London congregated at the Corn Exchange every Thursday. Mr Frank King, the custodian, recalled: "65 years ago, Broad Street used to be packed with people coming off the trains to the markets. Admission to the market cost farmers 3d [1p] a week, or 7s 6d [37p] a year", said Mr Harry Sale a Cambridge corn merchant whose association with the market started 41 years ago. Stand holders paid £3 5s [£3.25] a year, walking merchants – those who did not have stands – £1 6s [£1.30] a year, and merchants who visited occasionally 1s [5p] a week. While in the past sellers and buyers turned up in their hundreds, the average attendance in the last five or six years has dwindled to between 30 and 40. From next Thursday corn market activities are being transferred less than 100 yards across the street, to the club room at the rear of the Club Hotel. The Corn Exchange will continue in use for the time being for a variety of events. It has been the setting for dinners, political meetings, wrestling, boxing and darts tournaments. (News, 28 December 1962)

But it was not until July 1965 that the *News* could report: *Work is to start immediately on a block of lease-hold shops and offices on the former Corn Exchange site. The project will be carried out by Suburban Counties Properties Ltd of London who bought the site nearly 3 years ago for £20,000 and later demolished the Corn Exchange and adjoining cinema. The building work will be by J.H. Cross and Sons Ltd of Littleport; the architects are Fewster and Partners of London. The development is the third on what will become a 'new look' Market Place. Work on a new post office opposite the site started*

earlier this year while a supermarket at the junction with Brays Lane is nearing completion.

The shopping block containing four double and eight single shops and offices opened in 1966 but remained partially empty for two years, causing concern to traders who said it did not encourage new businesses or enhance the city centre. They were pictured by the *News* in August 1968. (neg 7982/P/37)

The architectural style of the development has attracted criticism for being out of character with the area – although an artist found the solution: leave it out! (neg 19269/P/6)

In May 1988 Coun Owen Bethell, Coun Michael Rouse and development manager Timothy Aldworth examined a new plan to guide development in Ely into the 21st century.

The Ely Local Plan sets out radical proposals to revamp the city. It includes setting aside land to build a new industrial estate between Cambridge Road and Witchford Road which could attract up to 2,000 jobs and building up to 1,500 homes on the outskirts of the city. Other proposals include building a new primary school near the proposed housing estate, restricting part of the city centre as a pedestrian area with the building of new car parks and creating a new multi-million pound shopping complex. Two London-based development companies are vying for the chance to build the new shopping centre on the cattle market site. Both propose to build a covered complex and make improvements to buildings in the nearby Market Square. Both schemes would involve demolishing and redeveloping the Post Office and one would also include knocking down and rebuilding the nearby Tesco stores. (News, 19 May 1988. neg 2465.88.19a)

The plan set out strict rules: *Garish designs for shops in Ely city centre will be outlawed in an attempt to save the area's character. The Market Square is full of neon signs, startling colours and 'horrendous' examples of new buildings merged with old which are spoiling the city's character, say planners. Now officers at East Cambridgeshire District Council have drawn up a new policy guide defining tasteful shop settings. Tim Aldworth, development manager, said Ely's historic character would disappear unless more careful thought was given to design. "There are one or two horrendous cases where shop fronts run across old buildings and totally ruin their appearance", he said. "It's too late to replace many of our historic buildings from the Market Square. They have already been replaced by modern design classics such as Tesco and the Post Office." Neon fascias should be replaced with hanging signs indicating the shop's purpose – for instance a boot pictured outside a shoe shop. Some shops were given a pat on the back by planners. An old-style shopping arcade along Club Mews was described as having tasteful traditional details and an attractive overall appearance. (News, 6 April 1991. neg 95181.9)*

A Tesco supermarket opened on the Market Place in October 1965 under its manager John Wilson. It would give employment to a staff of 35 men and women, recruited from the local area. The  building had been completed for over a year before Tesco moved in and work went on day and night to turn it into one of the most modern supermarkets in the country. There was 4,200 square feet of shop floor, with its own meat-preparation room, and freezers. For once the firm, always associated with progress and ultra-modern sales methods, had deferred to the old style, commented the *News*, Four years later the shop was extended to 7,000 square feet after becoming one of the fastest-growing branches anywhere in the country. The new extensions included a clothing and hardware section. It was officially opened in November 1969 by singer Vince Hill, who entertained hundreds of people with his hit song *Edelweiss*. (*News*, 7 March 1980. neg 807.80)

Other development had taken place nearby: *The site of the new Post Office in Market Place, Ely which will replace the existing Victorian building 100 yards away in Market Street. Work began earlier this year and the building is expected to be ready for occupation in the Autumn next year. The work will cost about £64,000. The site in Market Place, which has been vacant for some time, was once occupied by a Temperance Hotel. (News,* 31 July 1965. neg 3073/C)

The Post Office opened in October 1966. *The head postmaster, Mr A. Nix, his deputy, Mr A.J. East and about 50 members of staff will work for the first time in up-to-date offices designed to improve greater efficiency and pleasant working conditions. The office will accommodate six counter clerks, though should future developments require a larger public office, an allowance had been made for extending the rear. The office has been designed to give good natural light and acoustics. The ground floor has an aluminium 'house-style unit' treatment, which is to be standard for post offices throughout the country though as Ely is one of the first in the country to have this treatment the unit has been specially made. Among facilities included in the building are a writing room, accounts branch office, head and assistant postmasters' rooms, a loading bay for parcels and a kitchen where staff can cook their own meals* (News, 17 October 1966). Soon however the situation changed, by August 1969 the News reported: *Offices on the top floor of Ely's Post Office are to be converted into a flat. The Assistant*

Head Postmaster at Cambridge, Mr P.G. Croucher said: 'Now all the administrative work is done at Cambridge there are several offices at Ely, which are no longer of any use. We feel that by converting them into a flat we could bring in some revenue. (News, 22 August 1969. neg 13849/P/7)

The main Post Office subsequently closed and the site was redeveloped for the Cloisters shopping centre.

An earlier plan to enhance the area was the Club Mews. It was hailed by the *News* in June 1983: *It's always good when something old and unused is refurbished and put back into public use. This was the case when the Balsham-based firm of Bannerman developed part of the Old Club Hotel at Ely into a smart shopping precinct. The company opened up the Mews and stabling area and produced a smart precinct of small shops reminiscent of the early days*

when the hotel was built. The development which contains 17 shops, is reputed to have cost about £1 million and the precinct flourishes as an attractive trading area. (News, 30 June 1983. neg 2262.82.32)

The development did not thrive and was closed and redeveloped as part of the Cloisters shopping scheme.

The Cloisters shopping complex opened in November 1999: *The metal gates were pulled down for the public to see Ely's £5 million shopping complex. Now shoppers can wander through The Cloisters following its official opening and take a short cut through to Waitrose, but despite the red ribbon being cut, it will be at least two weeks before the first shop opened. Jon Higham, property manager for Aardvark Developments and Valerie Leake, vice chairman of East Cambridgeshire District Council, congratulated everyone involved in the scheme before declaring The Cloisters open for business. Mrs Leake said: "It is a splendid development which will breathe life into the city centre." Peacocks Stores will be the first shop to open in the 67,000 square foot complex. It is hoped Sportsworld and Card Fair will be open for Christmas trading. Wilkinsons, Iceland and Savers Health and Beauty will be open early next year, along with the new library. Four of the 10 units still have not been let, but the developers believe the centre will be full by the middle of next year. (News, 2 November 1999. neg 4409.99.22)*

The new Cloisters development brought new large shops into Ely: *Frozen food giant, Iceland, will welcome customers to its branch in the Ely shopping centre on April 4. Wilkinson, which sells home and garden products, will open on April 19. James Gibson, the manager of the new Iceland branch said: "I think the Iceland store will be a real asset to Ely." The new shop will create up to 16 new jobs. Jeff Young, Wilkinson branch manager said: "We really have had a fantastic response from the people of Ely to the news that Wilkinson is coming to town. The store will create 18 new full and part-time jobs, ranging from till assistants and cashiers to customer advice and security guards. (News, 28 March 2000. neg 2203M)*

The new shops face a Waitrose Supermarket and car park which occupy the site of what used to be a thriving Cattle and produce market: *Messrs A.T. Grain and Sons reported a record entry at their annual Fatstock Show at Ely. There were 44 cattle and 197 pigs on show. The judges – Messrs D.E. Leonard, Soham and A.S. Lemmon, Ely (cattle) and E. King, Ramsey (pigs) – said the standard was very high. The champion cup for the best fat steer or heifer went to a Hereford steer put in by Mr J. Wilson of Littleport, sold later at £12.2s.6d. per live cwt. The best pig was a Large White bacon which won the championship cup for Mr G.J. Johnson of Wicken. Mr D.R. Sulman of Witcham took the reserve championship with his Large White porker. (News, 20 December 1963. neg Y2946)*

The last auction of cattle and pigs at Ely livestock market was reported on 11 September 1981: *A 100-year-old tradition came to an end when cattle and pigs were auctioned at the last live-stock market held in Ely. During the past few years the market has had less business as more farmers switched from animals to arable farming, so the auctioneers who ran the market Cheffins, Grain and Chalk have decided to call it a day. It was a particularly sad day for the auctioneer, Mr John Grain, who first started work at the market exactly 48 years ago to the day. Before business started, Mr Grain, the third generation of his family to be involved in*

the market, said: "It's a sad day for me." He said the market was founded by his grandfather, Mr Arthur Trett Grain and continued under his father's guidance until he took over. At 10.45am Mr Grain rang the bell for the last time to summon farmers, dealers and onlookers to the final cattle sale. This time there was only one animal to be sold – a black Hereford brought along by Mr Sidney King, a Littleport farmer. It tipped the scales at 680kg and was bought by King Brothers of Holbeach, Lincolnshire for 100p a kilo. Then 78-year-old Mr 'Nips' Lee of Ely – a market hand for 63 years until he was forced to retire – was called to ring the bell to herald the start of the final pig sale. The bidding was brisk for the 50 pigs on offer, the last one being sold by Mr William Darby of Haddenham. Entering into the spirit of the occasion the bidders pushed the price up to 290p per kg, when it was bought by Mr Sidney King junior, of Littleport. (*News*, 11 September 1981. neg 3508.81.35)

The other part of the weekly market at Ely, the poultry, produce and furniture auctions continued for a while.

Pecks closed their city-centre hardware store, seen here in September 1991, relocating to new premises in Lisle Lane. (*News*, 23 September 1991. neg 6124.91.16)

Sometimes Fish'n'Chips are joined by even faster food: *Staff at Ely's Lamb Hotel used their experience to take top honours in the city's pancake races. The four-strong team beat off nine other sides to take the engraved frying pan presented to the winners by Ely's deputy mayor, Mr Brian Ashton. In the finals along Market Street, the Lamb team outran staff from Cutlack's, the city centre hardware store. The event was revived by Ely Leos, the junior division of the Lions Club after an absence of five years. They hope to raise more than £100 for cancer research and intend staging the event each year from now on. (News, 26 February 1990. neg : 1083.90.3a)*

Ely is fast becoming a thriving shopping centre. Every Thursday it has sprung to life for market day with farmers and other people from miles around congregating in the Market Square and taking advantage of the fact that some of the city pubs are open all day. Now Ely tends to be busy throughout the week. (News, 4 August 1977. neg 2173.77.27)

In September 1992 a street festival was held to celebrate the completion of the £500,000 pedestrianisation project in the city centre. The City of Ely Chamber of Trade and Industry organised the event which brought together a wide variety of craft and antique stalls, together with charity stalls and trade stands. Included in the entertainment line-up were buskers, face painters, morris dancers, Punch and Judy and the City of Ely band. There were exhibitions by craftsmen, including a blacksmith and a cooper who made barrels in the traditional fashion. The festival attracted large crowds. (*News*, 10 September 1992. neg 5922.92.23)

Market Street from the corner of Dolphin Lane, November 1989. At the start of the new decade city shopping was changing. The Co-op and the Post Office were closing, Tesco had moved to Broad Street and it would be a year before there was an in-town supermarket in the shape of Waitrose. (*News*, 10 December 1990. neg 6003.89.7)

The west side of the Market Place from the yard of the White Hart in March 1963. The Dolphin Inn on the corner of High Street closed in 1965 and the premises became an off-licence (*News* March 1963. neg Z3290)

The White Hart hotel was renovated in July 1963: *Stables built at the time when it was a coaching inn have been converted into a temporary public bar at the White Hart Hotel, Ely, which is undergoing extensive modernisation. Appropriately the licensee, Mr Alec Spencer, calls the conversion the "Stable Bar", though customers have been quick to name it "Bonanza" or "The Ponderosa" after a well-known television series. The whitewashed walls of the 85ft-long stables, latterly used as garages, have been faced with trellis work. The furniture comes from the hotel's original bar lounge. Mr Spencer expects normal facilities in the hotel to be restored by September, then he hopes to get the rooms, which accommodate many summer tourists, listed in a British travel catalogue.* (News, 6 July 1963. neg Z4179) The White Hart has now closed.

In October 1980 the *News* broke the story: *The only cinema in Ely, the Rex, will close if plans for a store on the site are approved. The owner, C and R Cinemas, has received a 'substantial' offer from Chaldondown Properties of Sutton near Peterborough which wants to knock it down and build a 11,000 square metre store in Market Street. The managing director of the C and R, Mr Tony Rowlett who runs two King's Lynn cinemas in partnership with Mr Malcolm Croot, blamed falling attendances and rising overheads for the decision. The cost of wages, rates and publicity had all increased tremendously, but audiences had not kept pace. Attendances were not helped by the fact that Ely was so close to Cambridge where the new films were shown.* (*News,* 23 December 1980)

Planning permission was granted in December 1980 for the demolition of the cinema, despite a petition containing 1,783 signatures opposing the plan: *The curtain came down at the weekend on the last picture show at Ely's doomed Rex Cinema. A large crowd of filmgoers turned up on Saturday night to see the last film, "Hawk the Slayer", screened at the Rex before it is demolished for a Boots store. The manager, Mr Bernard Brown said: "For many it was something of a sentimental visit. For everyone it was a sad occasion." The Rex is the only cinema left in a city which once boasted three.* (*News,* 5 January 1981. neg 20.81.9)

It was replaced by a new Boots chemist's shop.

Some parts of the city seem unchanging – as seen in this photograph taken in December 1979 although the Newday furniture shop closed in early 1982, and the Scotch Bakery followed. (*News*, 12 December 1979. neg 3415.79.17)

The names above the shops in High Street Passage have changed since this picture was taken in November 1990. (*News*, 9 November 1990. neg 6375.90.6)

The Woolpack Inn, a 200-year-old pub on the corner of Market Street and Newnham Street closed down in May 1969, when this picture was taken. The site was bought by the Tees Land Development Company Ltd of Stockton-on-Tees in March 1972 and work started on building a bank and offices. (*News*, May 1969. neg 12583/P/21)

Old Cottages in Newnham Street were the subject of controversy over plans to replace them with shops and offices in 1983. (*News*, 2 March 1983. neg 34.75.17a)

Changes continued: *Another Ely shop is closing down – the fourth this year. Rickwood and Sons, the furniture store in Newnham Street is to cease trading by the middle of the summer and the five staff are being made redundant. The firm's announcement comes hard on the heels of Theobald's decision to shut its High Street drapery and the closure of the Newday furniture shop a few yards away. The Ladybird children's boutique in Fore Hill is also now holding a closing-down sale. Rickwoods is the biggest shop to close so far. The manager, Mr Cyril Prior, said Rickwoods, a family firm which had been trading in Ely for nearly 100 years, had been forced to close because of ever-increasing costs.* (News, 26 May 1982. neg 1897.82.42)

Another big furniture store, Pettit's in Lynn Road, closed in March 1983.

But Ely gained new facilities. Plans were announced in February 1984 to convert the former Majestic Cinema into a snooker hall. They came to fruition in July 1986: *Brian and Nadine Smith are the couple behind the 147 Snooker Club and anyone who visited the one-time Majestic Cinema and later the bingo hall it became will be amazed at the transformation. The building has been gutted and totally refurbished. The old cinema balcony was dismantled and a new first floor built to accommodate four snooker tables. The ground floor also has four tables – each costing more than £4,000 – and the club is completed by a bar and lounge, nicely decorated and fully carpeted.* (News, 10 July 1986. neg 618.84.82)

In January 1969 the *News* could report work on the building of a new fire station in Egremont Street, at a cost of £35,000; the first part of the building was ready for occupation in September 1969. (*News*, 21 January 1969. neg 1568/R)

Firemen posing in front of the old building, September 1968. (*News*, 2 August 1968. neg 7218/P/25)

In January 1989 the *News* photographed Leading Fireman Richard White, Fireman Mike Pearson, Station Officer Gerry Walker and Firemen Dennis Pluck, Mick Jordan and John Foreman: *Ely firemen are the top of the Cambridgeshire ladder. The city's full-time fire crew has won the county's annual station efficiency award. The news has delighted the six full timers and their boss, Station Officer Gerry Walker, at the tiny station in Egremont Street. "We set ourselves a very high standard and it has paid off. It is a real team effort", he said. (News,* 26 January 1989. neg 341.89.28)

An open day at the fire station in September 1982 attracted an enthusiastic crowd of 400 people: *Old and new fire engines were on show at the Ely fire station open day. The city's new machine, which has only just entered service at the station, was on display alongside the vintage fire pumps from the adjoining museum. The station was open all afternoon with firemen manning stalls and side-shows and putting on a display of fire fighting. The day raised £142 for the Fire Service Benevolent Fund. (News,* 16 September 1982)

A view over the city centre, taken from the Cathedral in May 1986. (*News*, 19 May 1986. neg 2966.86.8)

A slight change of angle brings the Market Place into the picture taken during the rebuilding of the Corn Exchange and Post Office in April 1964. (neg Y6589)

Fore Hill, lined with a range of shops, pictured in 1979. *The centre of Ely is of course dominated by the Cathedral. But nestling around it in profusion are a variety of shops providing for virtually every need. Like every other town it has its traffic and parking problems. But they appear to be less severe in Ely. This enhances the area's attractiveness as a shopping centre. (News,* 12 December 1979. neg 3415.79.19)

Fore Hill drops steeply away, emphasised by the telephoto lens used for this 1977 photograph. (neg 2173.77.17)

Ye Olde Tea Rooms and Museum in Fore Hill closed in 1964. *The premises had been built in 1553 as a small house, but became a baker's shop at about the time Nelson lived. Frederick Thompson Cross acquired it in 1892 and 13 years later carried out extensive alterations to the shopfront overnight. For over half a century it housed a combined bakery, confectionery shop, restaurant and private museum with many articles displayed in cases, on the walls or hanging from the oak beams. The folk museum, acting as an adjunct to the restaurant attracted thousands of visitors. (News, 13 March 1964. neg Y5251)*

Vernon Cross was pictured with some of his collection just before it was auctioned in April 1964: *The auctioneer's gavel will seal the fate of pewter and brass, Staffordshire pottery and china, Elizabethan and 17-century fireplaces, early agricultural hand tools and equipment, mediaeval cooking cranes and fire jacks, clay pipes and smokers' requisites, firearms, swords and bayonets, Roman pottery, rush holders, books and documents. Mr F. Vernon Cross will nostalgically recall hundreds of weary miles trudging up and down muddy fen droves, and hours of back-aching digging at Roswell Pits. Mr Cross views the end of the museum quite philosophically: "One has to be a realist. It can't go on for ever." After over 50 years as a master baker and confectioner – though between the ages of 13 and 16 he toured the country as a ventriloquist and tumbler – he intends to retire as soon as he can sell his business. (News, 13 March 1964. neg Y5250)*

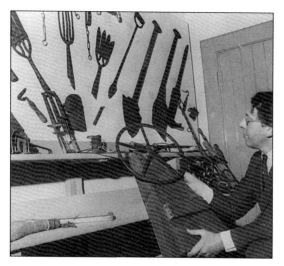

In 1975 a new museum opened – more than 20 years after it was first considered: *The museum, housed in the former choir school at The Sacrist's Gate, High Street, contains relics from the city and the surrounding area. Although mooted in the immediate post-war years it is only since the formation of the Ely Museum Society that definite steps have been taken to get the project off the ground. The former Ely Urban Council considered setting up a museum in the old gaol house in Lynn Road but the idea was shelved. About five years ago the museum idea was revived. Local architect, Mr Dennis Adams, held a public meeting and was inundated with support. From that meeting the Ely Museum Society was formed of which Mr Adams is now chairman. Most of the exhibits have been given or loaned by local people. (News, 1975. neg 1102.75.10a)*

The museum has now moved to magnificent premises at The Old Bishop's Gaol in Market Street.

One of the city's attractions for shoppers has been the availability of free parking. A large car park off Broad Street opened in 1965: *After opening Ely Urban Council's new £14,745 car park at the rear of Fore Hill, the chairman, Mrs B.O. Jefferson Smith, was driven round it in a 1925 Bullnose Morris Cowley. With her were the two other women councillors, Mrs E.M. Vinith-Williams, chairman of the Works Committee, and Mrs E.B. Cross. The car, owned by T.H. Nice and Co. Ltd., was driven from their Ely show rooms by Mr J.P. Stow, a director of the firm and manager at Ely. Mrs Jefferson Smith appealed to local motorists not to park in the streets all day but to use the new facilities and leave the short-stay car parks for visitors and shoppers from surrounding districts.The car park provides 107 spaces. The entrance is in Broad Street but a footpath connects with the top of Fore Hill and the city centre. (News, 15 March 1965. neg 8438B)* An extension was built the following year.

The Crin-O-Lite lampshade factory, in Broad Street was covered in a *News* 'Picture Parade' feature in December 1974. They found Mr Stan Baker and Mr Rex Nicklinson, directors of Crin-O-Lite, inspecting one of their products. (*News*, 19 December 1974. neg 2910.74)

Mrs Jean Green, Mrs Pat Williams and Mrs Grace Cullum assembling gimbles and pendants. (News, 19 December 1974. neg 2910.74.2). In July 1982 Tesco opened a new store in its place.

Further along Broad Street the former Three Blackbirds pub, believed to date back to the 13th century, was by 1983 in a very sad state. It became the subject of a major conservation project by the Ely Preservation Trust who announced plans to turn it into three homes. In the centre of the building they found a former open hall with a strutted crown roof, smoke blackened from open fires. In October 1984 the restored building was open after a three-year £100,000 project which had uncovered old beams, fireplaces and windows. (*News*, 10 February 1983. neg 489.83.1a)

The Cutter Inn was reopened in December 1964 after modernisation. *One of the new features is a public bar decorated as the interior of a ship's cabin and including a bar counter in the shape of a boat. The official opening was conducted by Stewart Morris, a former Olympic sailing gold medalist, who had known the Cutter since the 1930s when he practised on the Ouse as a member of the Cambridge University Sailing Club. He received the first pint of beer and downed it in one go.* (*News*, 11 December 1964. neg 4395B)

The Cutter enjoys a prime location: a view from the railway bridge in February 1989. (*News*, 23 February 1989. ncg 784.89)

The riverside area, photographed here in July 1983, has seen considerable change. (*News*, 21 July 1983. neg 2788.83.11a)

The Maltings, pictured in 1970, had been constructed to provide malt for the Ely brewery. It was badly damaged by fire and sold for £100 to the urban council on condition it be turned into a public hall. The proposal proved controversial with many favouring a centrally situated hall adjoining Paradise recreation ground, but the council decided to apply for permission to borrow £78,049 to meet the cost of the work and ask the County Council for a grant towards providing a public hall. The conversion work was undertaken by architect Mr Dennis Adams. The hardest job was the supporting of the roof and walls while two of the interior walls were removed. This produced a high oak-beamed hall lined with bare, sand-blasted, brick. The Maltings public hall was opened by the Secretary of State for the Environment Mr Peter Walker in October 1971. The scheme had cost £87,000. At the opening a member of the council of the Danish capital city of Ribe – Ely's sister city – presented a cheque for £25 to be spent on decorating the building. (*News*, 25 August 1970. neg 7310/P/29)

The Maltings restaurant, July 1995 shows how the scene has changed. (*News*, 20 July 1995. neg 4771.95)

Amongst the many functions the Maltings has hosted was a visit of BBC Television's *Antiques Road Show* in August 1979. *Arthur Negus and experts from leading auction houses were there to give valuations, together with Angela Rippon who presented the programme. Amongst the items brought in for assessment were items of local interest including a 12-foot punt gun made in 1840, which was probably used in the fens. Strapped to a boat and loaded with 30lb of shot it was capable of killing up to 200 birds at one go. The star of the show was a Ming vase valued by Hugo Morley-Fletcher at as much as £10,000. (News, 3 August 1979. neg 2032.79.13)*

Various improvements have taken place alongside the river to provide pedestrian access and additional moorings, seen here in July 1962. The Riverside Walk was formally opened in June 1968 by the chairman of the Ely Urban Council, Coun G.R. Mason. (*News,* 6 July 1962. neg Z1601)

The June calm of Waterside, 1965. (*News*, 9 June 1965. neg 1575C)

The river springs into activity in July for the Aquafest water carnival which attracts large crowds, as here in 1986: *Thousands of people flocked to Ely Aquafest, the city's annual river gala organised by the local Rotary Club. They enjoyed an afternoon of fun and entertainment including raft racing, a parade of floats, display by the Pathfinders Alsatian dog team, music from the City of Ely Military Band and disco dancing. Dozens of local clubs, charities and societies set up their own fund-raising stalls on the banks of the Ouse for the event, which was opened by the Mayor of Ely, Coun Ron Meadows. Organiser Myles Moffat said: "It's always difficult to estimate how many people attended, but we think we had 8,000-10,000. It was a great success, the weather was perfect for the event. Raft race winners were a team from Stiffkey in Norfolk, second were Greens' Sports and Social Club. The trophy for the best-decorated craft went to Ely RAF Hospital's floating aircraft.* (*News*, 7 July 1986)

Although many Aquafest competitors may end up in the river, children could enjoy themselves in Ely's outdoor swimming pool in Angel Drove, as here about May 1968. (neg 6345/P)

The 25-metre open-air pool was built by the old Ely Urban Council in 1934 and over the years had received a number of improvements, including the installation of heating. It passed into the ownership of East Cambridgeshire District Council in 1974. The site was sold by auction in November 1980, when it raised £13,000. The successful bidder was CHI Industries (UK), holding company of agricultural firm F.A. Standen and Sons (Engineering), which had its Hereward Works in Station Road, Ely. The 16,000 square feet site, covering a third of an acre, just over the road from the works would initially be used for storage. (*News*, 25 November 1980. neg 4357.80.15)

The old pool was replaced by a new heated covered pool at the Paradise Recreation Ground in New Barns Road. This was officially opened by British swimming star, Sharron Davies who complimented East Cambridgeshire District Council on the design of the £300,000 pool which incorporates energy-saving features, under-water lighting and special provisions for the disabled. As Miss Davies opened the pool 20 children from all over East Cambridgeshire dived in for the first official swim. (*News*, 2 June 1981. neg: 2378.81.24)

Angel Drove, on the right, has become an area of considerable new development. In October 1975 Keymarkets announced plans for a 2,000 square feet fresh food supermarket in Ely. It applied for planning permission for the change of use of three factory units on the Angel Drove industrial estate into a supermarket. The supermarket could be on the scale of the new Superkey store at Wisbech and would be intended to serve shoppers living in a ten-mile radius. Opposition to the proposals came from the East Cambridgeshire District Council who felt traffic flow would create problems and that such a complex would draw away trade from other shops in Ely. A new draft plan for Ely town centre was due to be considered soon and any decision to allow the supermarket could be in opposition to conclusion of the plan. Ely Chamber of Trade were not afraid of a superstore if it were in the city centre. An inquiry in November 1976 was warned that Ely was in danger of falling behind other towns in the 'shopping revolution'; the proposed store was not a

hypermarket, but would be mainly selling groceries and would attract people who were now shopping in the Superkey store at Wisbech and Sainsbury's, Cambridge. The scheme was rejected by the Department of the Environment in January 1977 since it would lead to closure of smaller shops and this would be socially undesirable where village shops, post offices and the like were affected. (*News*, 1981. neg 951.81.16)

In 1994 Tesco opened a new superstore in Angel Drove to replace its Broad Street store. It was opened by Malcolm McGowan who had worked for the company for some 30 years. Nearby an industrial park was established alongside a new bypass road running through to the A10, seen here in October 1996. (*News*, 1 October 1996)

Ely station freight distribution area, photographed by well-known Ely photographer, Walter Martin Lane.

Ely Railway Station itself was voted one of the best kept in the region in May 1982 when the *News* photographed the manager Arthur Suckling (left) with some of his staff. (*News*, 20 May 1982. neg: 1734.82.42)

In January 1964 the *News* photographers joined the 'Grunty Fen Express' on its journey between Ely and Sutton. The line opened to Sutton in 1866 and was later extended as far as St Ives. It carried its last regular passengers in 1931, though special excursion trains continued to run. It closed completely in July 1964.

Once a day at 1.15pm the little diesel train leaves Ely station, goes eight miles and arrives at Sutton. Then at 3.20 pm it turns round and goes back again. Hauling three goods wagons it stops first at Little Thetford – where the driver and fireman nip down smartly from the cab, open and close the gates, and continue the trip. The train takes less than an hour for the journey, carrying mainly fuel, with possible stops at Stretham, Wilburton and Haddenham. (*News*, 30 January 1964)

The fireman, Mr Robert Gilbey of Cambridge and Mr Jack Watson, of Ely, open the level crossing gate at Little Thetford (now long since removed). (neg Y4063)

Arriving at Haddenham station (neg Y4060)

The train leaves Sutton station on the return journey. (neg Y4065)

The crossing gates at Ely station have been modernised since this photograph was taken in September 1969, but the underpass has remained the same height. As vans and lorries have become taller numerous incidents have occurred in which vehicles have become wedged. (*News*, September 1969. neg 13965/P/12)

The old Ely High Bridge, across the Ouse, was replaced in April 1982, just a year after this picture was taken. (*News*, 2 March 1981. neg 814.81.13)

Ely Cathedral

Often traffic builds up along the Stuntney road while large lorries wait for the crossing gates to open. Travellers are compensated by this view of the Cathedral across the flood plain, taken in February 1994. (*News*, 15 February 1994. neg 882.94.21)

Ely Cathedral attracts thousands of visitors, some of whom now arrive by foot along the long distance Fen Rivers Way footpath, but in March 1969 it was the start of a 20-mile walk by members of the Ely Round Table to raise money for a mini-bus. All but one of the 21 walkers completed the course from Ely to Stretham, Wicken, Soham and Stuntney. The Ely Palace School provided a nurse to bandage sore feet on the way round. (*News*, 3 March 1969. neg 1740/R)

Autumn in Ely and Ken Long sweeps up leaves on Palace Green, 1970. (*News*, 6 November 1970. neg 18802/P/9)

In June 1981 Palace Green was crowded with 2,500 schoolchildren from 22 schools who re-enacted the building of the Cathedral to celebrate the ninth centenary of its construction. The pageant began with a depiction of the arrival of St Etheldreda in 673. (*News*, 25 June 1981. neg 2421.81.11a)

The Queen visited Ely in November 1973 at the culmination of the 13th centenary of the foundation of a monastery at Ely by St Etheldreda. *She dressed for the weather in a fitted coat of white wool trimmed with brown fur and a brown hat with white fur. She looked charming, cosy and every inch a Queen as she paused to meet pupils of the Palace School.* (*News*, 23 November 1973. neg 9840.11a)

Her Majesty visited Ely Cathedral again in 1987 to distribute the Royal Maundy. A congregation of 2,600 people attended the service when 61 men and 61 women, one for each of the Queen's life, received the coins in appreciation of their service to the church or the community. Afterwards accompanied by the Bishop of Ely, she met residents of the Tower Hospital and Sue Ryder Home in front of Palace Green (*News*, 16 April 1987. neg 1458.87.23)

In November 1993 the Queen returned to view some of the £4 million restoration work which had been carried out since 1986. Then at the Sue Ryder Home she was presented with a bouquet and met Lady Ryder of Warsaw together with volunteer workers in her international charity. (*News*, 26 November 1993. neg 7899.93.22)

The unprecedented period of renovation and repair included work on the painted ceiling of the nave where conservators cleaned off a century of grime to reveal the true beauty of the magnificent paintings beneath. (*News*, 11 April 1988. neg 1828.88.14)

Above the ceilings work continued on the roof and stonework. In March 1988 the Cathedral's restoration appeal received a £3,000 boost from Kries Viersen, Cambridgeshire's twin region in West Germany: *The donation, given as part of celebrations to mark the fifth anniversary of the twinning link, was handed over to the Dean, the Very Revd Bill Patterson after a special evensong. The Dean said the cash would be used to help restore the east wall and the visitors were shown where work is to be done. He said the appeal fund now stood at £4,045,000 with an additional £70,000 in the 21st century fund, set up to finance regular maintenance once restoration is completed.*

The picture shows the Very Revd Bill Patterson showing the German visitors around the roof work at the Cathedral. (*News,* 22 March 1988. neg 1557.88.25a)

Work on the Lady Chapel was underway in April 1989: *Not since Victorian times has the Cathedral undergone such a major facelift. A total of £1.7 million is being spent on phase one alone. More than 40 craftsmen employed by Cambridge building firm Rattee and Kett, supervised by site agent Mr Roy Blunt and cathedral architect Mr Peter Miller are already two thirds of the way through the project. At the end of the month they will start on phase two, the restoration of the Lady Chapel, the east wall of the presbytery and the north choir aisle. Phase three – the final project – will involve work on the south transept, the south west transept and the west tower.* (*News,* 11 April 1988. neg 1761.89.16a)

The completed restoration was celebrated with a visit by the Duke of Edinburgh in October 2000. Since 1986 £12 million had been spent to ensure the building's survival into the next century.

The Cathedral now houses a Stained Glass Museum, visited by Princess Margaret in May 1980. She showed great interest in the workshop at the end of the museum gallery where Mr Geoffrey Carrick and Mr Peter Lister, stained glass craftsmen from Norwich, demonstrated methods of cleaning, restoring and strengthening glass. (News, 16 May 1980. neg 1454.80.36)

Princess Margaret visited the Cathedral again in July 1997 to open a flower festival.

A radiant Princess Margaret officially opened Ely Cathedral's spectacular Flower Festival. Thousands of flowers have transformed the Ship of the Fens into a blaze of colour from floor to ceiling. An excited crowd of about 200 people waited outside the Cathedral to catch a glimpse of the Princess. She was in a relaxed mood as she admired the 300 arrangements on the theme "The Power and the Glory", which a dedicated army of 500 talented arrangers from East Anglia had skilfully displayed. The Dean, the Very Revd Michael Higgins, paid tribute to the flower festival designer Sue Brinton and her dedicated band of helpers. This is the third flower festival to be held at the Cathedral. Diana, the Princess of Wales, opened the last one which took place 10 years ago. Members of the City of Ely Flower Club were delighted that the royal visitor had stopped to admire the 6,000 blooms which they had arranged in a mosaic design on the floor. Judith Underwood of Bentham Way, Ely, said: "I think she was overawed by it all. I don't think she expected to see what was in here." (News, 10 July 1997. neg 5602.97.12a)

Improved heating ensures that visitors are given a warmer welcome than ever before. In March 1964 the News snapped Mr William Pomfret tending the Cathedral stoves. (*News*, 24 March 1964. neg Y5856)

The Cathedral's religious work has adapted to meet changing circumstances: *When the Rt Revd Robert Arnold Schurhoff Martineau became Suffragan Bishop of Huntingdon he was the first man to hold an office originally created nearly 430 years ago. His commissioning in Ely Cathedral was watched by more than 300 people. They heard the Bishop of Ely, the Rt Revd E.J.K. Roberts say: "There has been a Suffragan Bishop of Huntingdon since 1538. The Church of England sets about its business with caution and it has taken nearly 430 years to be sure of the right man." For the commissioning cathedral clergy and the Bishop of Ely, preceded by the choir of St John's church, Cambridge, walked in procession to the Octagon. There, in front of the nave altar the coped and mitred Bishop Martineau, escorted by the archdeacons, stood as the seated Bishop of Ely read the document of commission and handed him his crosier. Then, following cathedral statutes the Suffragan Bishop was conducted to the choir gates where, after the administration of the canonical oath, he was installed by the Dean of Ely, the Very Revd C.P. Hankey. After the service the new Bishop of Huntingdon blessed the congregation.* (News, 17 January 1966. neg 7975/C)

More than 300 youngsters attended the annual Christingle service at Ely Cathedral and raised £350 for the work of the Church of England Children's Society. They took purses containing donations for the society which they presented to the Bishop of Huntingdon, the Rt Rev Gordon Roe and then each received Christingles – oranges decorated with a ribbon, candle and fruit, part of a centuries-old Moravian custom. (News, 17 December 1988. neg 6601.88.25)

Some of the congregation howled and barked when the organist started to play the first hymn during a service at Ely Cathedral. Others let out yelps and growls that echoed around the mighty Norman building. A few even managed to doze despite the racket while others munched contentedly wondering what all the fuss was about. The vice-dean, Canon Dennis Green, used a microphone to make himself heard to the rest of the congregation. No one minded about the chaos because all were taking part in a blessing service for animals and owners, thought to be the only one of its kind in the country. It was organised by the Dean and Chapter in conjunction with Wood Green Animal Shelters following the success of a similar event last year. Hundreds of people took animals of all shapes and sizes to the service – cats, dogs, sheep, goats, ponies, donkeys, pigs and cows. (News, 18 April 1988. neg 1957.88.8a)

The Cathedral choir plays an essential part in the services; in 1968 they adopted new robes: *Choristers of Ely Cathedral are now wearing new-style robes. On the left John Minett shows the new style which is similar to a monk's habit, contrasting with the old style worn by Malcolm Sugar. (News, 14 May 1968. neg 1470/D)*

Other choirs from around the world also participate from time to time.

Canon George Youell, the Cathedral treasurer, shows an American choir of St Michael and All Angels, Georgia, around the Cathedral where they are singing at services this week. It is the second time the choir has sung at the Cathedral. Their own church seats 200 people. (News, 2 August 1972. neg 5057.26a)

The Cathedral has been the venue for many important services. Here members of the Ely Diocesan Mothers' Union arrive for a service to dedicate a new banner in March 1962. (*News*, 15 March 1962. neg K8513)

In May 1965 members of the British Legion gathered for a very special service: *A once-in-a-lifetime event was how the area secretary, Mr E.B. Macgregor of Cambridge summed up the Eastern area British Legion Rally and parade at Ely. The city, scene of many parades in the past, had never seen anything like it. Long before the rally was timed to start 160 coaches and cars in their hundreds converged on the city. Out of them spilled nearly 7,000 legionnaires almost doubling the population from counties in the eastern area. About 3,750 of them went to assembly points from which, joined by 15 bands, they marched to the Cathedral. Inside every available inch was used for seating by the congregation. As they sang the opening hymn the Queen's old standard, being paraded for the last time, was handed to the Dean of Ely, the very Revd C.P. Hankey, for laying-up in the Cathedral. The new standard was unfurled and dedicated by the Bishop of Ely. Outside hundreds who had listened to loudspeakers relaying the service saw the new standard head the long parade covering three decades of British military history and three generations of ex servicemen. Mr Macgregor said: "I shall be surprised if ever there is another parade like this in the area." (News, 24 May 1965. neg 890/C/34)*

Not all services pass without a hitch: *Police were called to Ely Cathedral to eject a woman who staged a demonstration during the Remembrance Day service. Retired Wing Commander John Grant, president of the Ely Royal British Legion, said that despite the incident the service and the parade was one of the best. (News, 14 November 1988. neg 5916.88.18)*

In August 1990 a march past of men and women of the Royal Air Force followed a special service in the Cathedral to celebrate the 50 anniversary of the Ely RAF Hospital. (News, 7 August 1990. neg 4738.90.20)

Ely Hospitals

The hospital had been founded in a former convalescent home at Littleport in September 1939 and moved to Ely the following year. In April 1968 the News reported: *At one minute past midnight Ely RAF Hospital became a station of Strike Command, the RAF's new principal front-line organisation. To mark the birth of the new structure there was a colour-hoisting parade at the hospital today. Strike command has been created by the merger of Fighter Command to which the hospital belonged and Bomber Command, both of which were formed in July 1936. The salute was taken by the Commanding Officer, group Captain T.N.N. Brennan. (News,* 30 Apr 1968. neg 6267/P/4a)

The Hospital's exterior remained relatively unchanged, the News using a picture from 1968 to report welcome news in 1980: *A major expansion scheme expected to cost nearly £4 million is planned for Ely RAF Hospital. Four operating theatres, two new wards and a number of other facilities are to be added. The expansion – brought about by the decision to close the RAF Hospital at Nocton Hall, Lincolnshire – will mean a significant increase in the number of civilian and service jobs.From 1983 Ely will be the RAF's only hospital in the Eastern Counties and the new facilities will be needed to cope with the extra number of in-patients. The present hospital has 142 beds in seven wards and two new wards are to be added as part of the expansion scheme. Four new operating theatres will be built to replace the two existing ones which will be converted for other uses. A new physiotherapy unit, gymnasium and remedial therapy centre will be added and the size of the dental clinic will be increased. A number of old buildings are to be demolished and their facilities relocated in the main buildings. The hospital already takes National Health Service patients in the area but the spokesman was unable to say whether their numbers would be increased after 1983. (News,* 16 January 1980. neg 9411/P/25, taken October 1968)

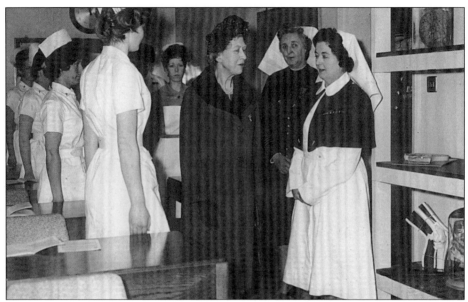

Earlier improvements had come in April 1963 when the Princess Royal opened a new out-patient department. In the morning she inspected the Officers' Quarters, the Nurses' Training School where she spoke to student nurses, and Airmen's Dining Room before lunching in the Officers' Mess and touring the wards. (*News*, 23 April 1963. neg Z7827)

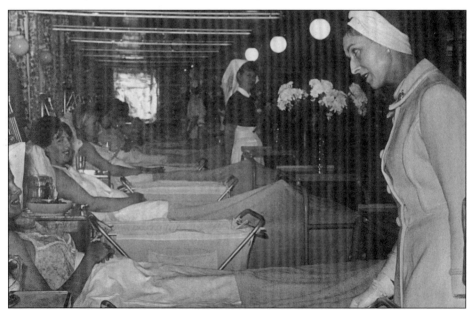

Other Royal visits followed: Princess Alexandra paid an official visit to the Hospital in May 1971 when she toured four of the wards – maternity, children's, men's surgical and women's medical. She was also introduced to 61-year-old Miss Doris Lambert who has been a domestic cleaner and bat-woman at the hospital for 30 years. (*News*, 28 May 1971. neg 1021/22)

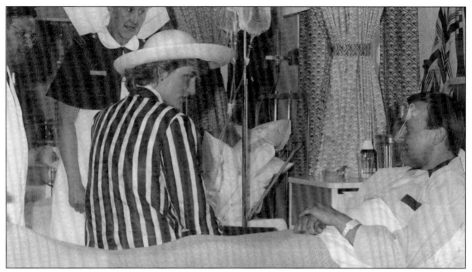

In July 1987, Diana, Princess of Wales, visited the Hospital, which was renamed in her honour. She met both service and civilian patients including Corporal William Lownds during her visit to the surgical ward. *The Princess captivated everyone with her beauty and charm during her visit to Ely and the hospital was her first stop. Wearing a navy blue and white striped silk suit, she arrived to cheers of welcome at the 168-bed hospital. She thrilled the crowds with chats during an informal walkabout which put her way behind schedule after opening a three-day flower festival in the Cathedral. (News, 10 July 1987. neg 2905.87.17)*

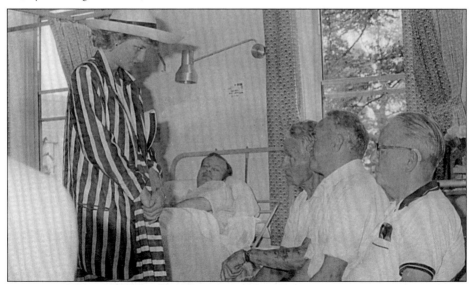

Three men who were virtually blind had a perfect view of the Princess of Wales during her visit to Ely – 24 hours after an operation to restore their sight. Ronald Jakes of Prickwillow, Charles Few from Cromer and Squadron Leader Jim Hickie of Brampton met the Princess as she toured the Hospital. Mr Jakes said: "One day my eyesight was terrible, the next I could see clearly. What an honour to be able to see and meet the Princess of Wales. (News, 10 July 1987. neg 2905.87.29)

In January 1987 the *News* pictured Group Captain John Baird, the new Commanding Officer of RAF Hospital, Ely being welcomed by the previous Commanding Officer, Group Captain Jim Greig. But changes were in the air and closure was announced. The last RAF patient left in July 1992 and the hospital passed to Cambridge Health Authority as a community hospital after a considerable campaign by residents to keep a hospital facility in Ely. Baird Lodge, a new sheltered housing development was opened nearby. (*News,* 7 January 1987. neg 4587.13)

The Tower Hospital played an important part in the life of the community. In June 1976 a new day hospital, catering for 15 elderly people, was dedicated by the Bishop of Huntingdon, the Rt Revd Eric Wall, seen talking to Mrs Hagare King and Mr George Nottage. The centre provided physiotherapy to help patients regain the use of their limbs, speech therapy and occupational therapy. The Friends of Tower Hospital contributed towards its facilities. (*News,* 9 June 1976. neg 1663.76.7)

By April 1990 the Tower Hospital, a former Victorian workhouse, was beyond economic repair. The hospital's manager, Mr Colin Vincent said, "The staff are providing the highest standards of clinical care in appalling surroundings and we need to do something about that for them and for patients." The Tower Hospital officially closed in May 1993 when 62 elderly patients were taken to their new home at the refurbished Princess of Wales Hospital in a fleet of ambulances and minibuses. The old hospital was sold. (*News*, 13 May 1993. neg 424.83.11)

Hospital Sunday has become a traditional part of the calendar: *Thousands of spectators lined the streets of Ely for the city's record-breaking Hospital Carnival parade. They helped raise £3,835 – more than ever before – for the old folks at the city's Tower Hospital. More than 50 floats together with bands and majorettes took part in the 29th annual parade organised by the Friends of the Hospital. The parade toured part of Ely, then stopped for a united church service on St Mary's Green before winding round the rest of the city. The Friends chairman, Mr Ken Howard, said he was 'over the moon' with the success of the event, which raised £3,200 last year. (News, 30 May 1989. neg 2720.89.3)*

Other 'traditions' are of more recent origin: *Heavy rain failed to dampen the spirits of pupils at the King's School, Ely, who turned out in force for the annual hoop trundle. Despite the weather the entire school cheered on the 25 competitors who took part in the sixth trundle event in the Cathedral precincts. The winners were 17-year-old Neil Emerson and Elizabeth Vigrass, aged 18. Each received hand-made wooden tankards given to the school as perpetual trophies for the trundle. It derives from a custom dating back to the Middle Ages when the school's pupils were allowed to spin their tops and trundle hoops in the Cathedral if the weather was bad. The tradition was revived in 1979. (News, 26 March 1984. neg 1229.84.36)*

The King's School is housed in the shadow of the Cathedral, and when the sun shines sometimes takes its lessons outside in the park. (neg 4929)

Ely Schools

The King's School has continued to flourish: Headmaster Hubert Ward welcomed an important visitor in May 1989: *A £1.5m improvement scheme to the King's School, Ely, was opened by Mr Michael McCrum, vice-chancellor of the University of Cambridge. The scheme has seen the building of new facilities and the refurbishment of existing buildings and has taken 10 years to complete. Builders finished the final section, new buildings to house day boys, nine classrooms and a sixth-form common room last year. Earlier parts of the scheme included accommodation for girls, and the conversion of the roof space in the old Hereward building to provide careers and examination department along with offices and meeting rooms. The physical science building was completely refurbished and a further floor was added at a cost of almost £250,000. (News, 13 May 1989. neg 2212.89.19a)*

More money has been spent on the Bishop's Palace to fund its conversion to a new Sue Ryder home: *Contracts for the conversion of the Old Palace building into a new Sue Ryder Home at Ely were*

officially handed over in October 1990. The conversion would treble the capacity of the existing home for the incurably ill, and bring the total of beds to 42. At the ceremony were, (from left) Judy Maud, Bishop Stephen Sykes, Rattee and Kett contracts manager Grant Barker, Brian Ashton, appeal director Timothy Finn, matron of the Old Palace Home Patsy Woodhead, Dr Ian Nichol and Sarah Dani (architect). (News, 12 October 1990. neg 5874.90.11)

The building had previously been home to the Palace School, an independent charity run under the guidance of the British Red Cross Society since 1946. It closed in summer 1983 despite a determined campaign to save it. At that time it had only 20 pupils and costs were too high. In 1981 the *News* reported: *There is no lack of demand for Ely Palace School dancing team, which is often called on to give displays for clubs and societies in Cambridgeshire. Nothing unusual about that one might think – many schools have dance teams. But the Palace School caters for the physically handicapped and the remarkable thing about its dancers is that they perform in wheelchairs. The wheelchair dancing team was formed in the summer term of 1977 and has gone from strength to strength. The display team consists of eight members. For them it is a valuable hobby which helps them meet dozens of new friends among the women's clubs, school and local fetes where they perform. But the team is also very competitive, winning the national wheelchair dancing championship in 1978. The 12 main members are: Akram Lari, Natasha Handscomb, Karen Doughty, Caroline French, Paul Granville, Kim Palmer, Colin Walker, Paul Panter, Leslie Graves, Steven Smith, Terence Boyle and Mark Alce. The dance teacher is Mrs Susan Yates. The children wear specially designed evening costumes made by the school's seamstress, Mrs Ellen Brown. Displayed on the back of each wheelchair is the school's emblem.* (News, 19 March 1981. neg 889.81.12)

There have been changes in other special needs provision: *The Headmistress of Ely's Highfield School which is now under threat of closure hit back at critics who claimed her buildings are inadequate. A County education working party had said the school should be closed down and pupils sent to Wisbech and Cambridge for special education. But headmistress, Mrs Dorothy Womack said the buildings were of recent origin and with the help of an active parent group the school was well-equipped particularly with special aids for enabling youngsters with standing and balance difficulties to derive more benefit from their education. The ages of Highfield children range from six to 18. "In a school of this nature where you are dealing with different handicaps, you cannot group children chronologically",* she said. (News, 5 November 1981. neg 4279.81.24)

After a 10-year concerted campaign it was reprieved and in 1997 moved to the Sixth Form Centre at the City of Ely College where it would be able to take 100 pupils.

Other pupils had also moved onto the site: *Primary schoolchildren going to Ely Community College in September have spent three days getting to know their new school. The 200 pupils followed a normal school timetable and attended lessons in readiness for entering secondary school in the new academic year. The idea behind the scheme is to familiarise the pupils with their new school so they know what to expect – and are not lost when they arrive. Principal Dr Carole Stroud said: "The pupils loved it – they always do. It is lovely to see them coming in." Most of the pupils come from St Mary's Junior School, St Joseph's Junior School, Downham Feofees, Littleport Village College or Littleport Millfield schools. (News, 8 July 1999. neg 2793.99.10)*

Pupils from an earlier generation – students of Ely High School for Girls at speech day, 1965. (*News*, 29 October 1965. neg 2616B)

It was an emotional occasion: *For Dr Bertha Tilly yesterday's Ely High School speech day was her last. She retires next year after 30 years as headmistress. In a tribute to Miss Tilly, the chairman of the governors, Mr J.M. Sneesby, said: "It is a very fine record. By her force of character, devotion and hard work she has built up a school of which we are all proud." In her speech Miss Tilly made a plea for the preservation of grammar school standards in any educational reorganisation plan. She said "Plans are already afoot which may, if put into action, cause this school to lose its identity." (News, 29 October 1965. neg 2615B)*

The High School became part of the City of Ely College under a new comprehensive set-up in September 1972.

Amongst other educational changes the *News* has reported: *The headmistress and founder of the Acremont School, Ely, Mrs Marion Saunders, retired in July 1982. The school has been bought by the King's School but will continue to be run separately. Three hundred former pupils, parents and friends gathered to say farewell and to present Mrs Saunders with a £1,000 cheque. Mrs Saunders started the school in 1949 at Back Hill. Ely, with eight pupils. But she soon moved into the present building in Egremont Street. Now the school has about 120 pupils, aged between four and 11. "I feel sad about leaving, but fulfilled", she said. Mrs Saunders and her husband, a retired teacher, are moving to Barton Mews for their retirement. Also retiring from the school is Mrs Lorna Abbott, who has taught there for 23 years. The new headmistress will be Mrs Patricia Kreyer. (News, 10 July 1982. neg 2481.82.17)*

Headmistress of Ely Primary School, Miss Sally Lawson, holds a basket of names for Anouska Gregorek and Tristan Ffitch to draw the names of the two pupils who will open the school. The school was established in September 1985 when St Audrey's and St Etheldreda's were amalgamated as part of an educational shake up in Ely. The lucky pupils were Warwick Brown and Joanne Abbs. (*News*, 19 March 1986. neg 1077.86.5)

"Operation Switchover", the transfer of equipment, mostly books, from the Ely St Mary's Church of England Junior School in St Mary's Street to the new £90,000 buildings at High Barns, was completed yesterday. And 50 boys in the top form had time off lessons to help load the books into the removal van that provided a shuttle service between the two schools. All the pupils have taken part in "Operation Switchover." The headmaster, Mr Walter Bebbington, said: "The idea was to let them become involved in the move." The school have used St Mary's Street for three years. They moved in when the Needham's School transferred to their new buildings in Downham Road. Before that they were in separate buildings in Silver Street and Broad Street. (*News*, 20 July 1971. neg 1473.10)

Out-of-school play provision has been improved: *Youngsters throughout Ely have cleaner and brighter play areas – thanks to the efforts of mothers and the generosity of the local council. Several parks around the city have been upgraded and improved following an energetic campaign by mums who formed the Play Safe Ely Group. Seven areas have been re-equipped by architects Hereward Design and the work was paid for by the District Council. The revamped play areas were opened by Coun John Seaman, vice-chairman of East Cambridgeshire District Council, Coun Owen Bethell chairman of the council's recreation and tourism panel and the Mayor of Ely Coun Walter Bebbington, seen here at the St John's Road playground. (News, 1 Feb 1994. neg 536.94.4a)*

But nothing can beat the fun nature provides: Ely youngsters make the most of the winter snow on Cherry Hill near Ely Cathedral, January 1985. (*News*, 12 January 1985. neg 80.85.53)

On the top of Cherry Hill, stands a largely unknown memorial erected in 1779 by James Bentham, a canon of the Cathedral. *Two years of hard work were toasted in wine and cherries when the Ely Society celebrated the restoration of the Bentham Memorial on Cherry Hill, Ely. When restoration started the memorial had been demolished by vandals and lay in pieces But with the help of £600 in grants, Ely builder Mr John Ambrose restored it to its former glory while conservation volunteers cleared the spiralling path to the summit. (News,* 22 August 1985. neg 3267.85.81)

Agriculture

Dominating the skyline to the north was the Ely Sugar Beet Factory established in 1925.

A bumper crop is expected at Ely sugar beet factory this season where staff are preparing to process more than half a million tons of beet. The 200 shift workers and 140 day workers expect to make over 62,000 tons of sugar during the next four months. Unlike most of the other sugar factories Ely does not produce the finished product, but sends over 500 tons of raw sugar daily in bulk to other factories or refineries. Farmers, mainly in the cattle-rearing areas, take most of the 40,000 tons of molassed pulp produced in an average season. (News, September 1963. neg Y1367)

Improvements continued to be made: *A new labour-saving plan installed this year includes an automatic centrifugal for spinning sugar from the syrup, to replace two old ones and a large vacuum pan for boiling the syrup, which will supplant two smaller and less efficient ones. The new pan will give greater capacity than the other two together. (News, 15 September 1966. neg 5211/D)*

Operating machinery at the factory, January 1967. (neg 9126)

The factory also provided work for transport companies: *The first of the fleet of lorries that in the next four months will make thousands of journeys rolled into the Ely Beet Sugar Factory at the start of another sugar processing campaign. By next January when the non-stop campaign ends the factory expects to have dealt with around 456,000 tons of sugar beet.* (*News*, 1 October 1970. neg 18448/P)

Farmers needed to invest in new equipment to harvest the beet: *Demonstration of the new Standen Ltd sugar beet harvester alongside a normal tractor-pulled harvester interested visitors who watched it in action near Ely.* (*News*, 16 September 1964. neg 1570B)

Old ways have changed, though heavy horses continued to be used on Cole Ambrose's farm at Stuntney for many years; here beans are harvested in October 1968. (*News*, 5 October 1968. neg 9011/P/23a)

Potatoes being harvested on a field at Sidney Farm, Prickwillow, 1974. (neg 3049.74.17a)

In the fields hard manual work continues: hoeing peas at C.N. Starling's farm, Littleport. (*News*, 14 May 1965. neg 620/C)

Celery picking at Prickwillow in a field belonging to Hopkins Farm, 1974. (*News*, 1 November 1974. neg 3049.74.10a)

Now the procedure is more mechanised: harvesting iceberg lettuces on Shropshire's Stretham farm, 1991. (*News*, 28 May 1991. neg 2925.91.6)

Lettuces are sorted and packed in the field on giant machines. (*News*, 28 May 1991. neg 2629.01.12)

Little gem lettuce and celery are sorted at the pack house at Shropshire's farm, Barway. (*News*, 28 May 1991. neg 2626.91.12)

Land work has always been poorly paid: *Farm workers and their families marched in protest through the centre of Ely to highlight their national pay claim for £140 a week. More than 100 workers from Cambridgeshire and surrounding counties joined the march – believed to be the first trade union rally held in the city. En route from the Ship Lane car park to the Centre E youth club, they stopped at the Cambridgeshire headquarters of the National Farmers' Union in Broad Street where they handed a letter to the county secretary, Mr Derek Crawley. (News, 9 March 1987. neg 904.87.11)*

Roads

Life can be hard in the bleak black fenland and many now commute to work in Cambridge. (neg 1562/74/15a)

The journey time has been reduced through road improvements: the Minister for Road and Traffic, Mr Peter Bottomley at the opening of the £8 million Ely and Littleport Bypass which he described as a 'a much needed road." With him are, from left, Coun Keith Leonard, Chairman of Cambridgeshire County Council, Coun Mike Rouse, chairman of East Cambridgeshire District Council, Coun Ron Barber chairman of Littleport Parish Council, the Mayoress of Ely, Mrs Pat Meadows and the Bishop of Ely. (*News*, 25 June 1986. neg 3494.86.22)

Road improvements being carried out at a cost of £74,000 on a one-mile stretch of A10 at Little Thetford, April 1968 – though residents are now campaigning for a roundabout. (*News*, 23 April 1968. neg 5537/P)

A new bypass was constructed at Stretham, with a new bridge at Stretham Ferry replacing a dangerous bend: *The Department of the Environment has accepted the £293,449 tender for the work from Cambridge firm D and H Contractors. The scheme is expected to be completed in 15 months. The scheme, which has been designed by Cambridgeshire's County Surveyor, Mr Robert Lacey, will cut out the present sharp bend in the road where it crosses the River Ouse. It will involve diverting the road to the west from points about 250 yards either side of the present bridge. A new bridge will be built where the river joins Chear Lode. A statement issued by the Department of the Environment says the present bridge is deteriorating and the bend on the approach to the bridge restricts visibility and is a potential hazard to traffic and pedestrians. In the past a number of accidents, including at least one fatal, have*

occurred at or near the bridge. When the diversion is complete the existing road and bridge will be kept as a service road for the riverside and the public house at the bridge. (*News*, 23 July 1975. neg 2029/75/10)

The new road opened in August 1976, five months ahead of schedule.

VILLAGES ARE ENDURING YET EVER-CHANGING PLACES, AS THE NEWS HAS REPORTED OVER THE YEARS

Coveney and Wardy Hill

A new hand-carved village sign for Coveney was unveiled by the Mayor of Ely, Coun. Henry Constable. The sign has been bought by the Coveney Women's Institute and was carved by Mr Harry Carter of Swaffham, Norfolk, who has designed and made dozens of signs for East Anglian villages. The sign was formally handed over to the chairman of the parish council, Mr John Fyfe, by the WI president, Mrs Dorothy Duffield. The £135 for the sign had been raised mainly from a bazaar held in the village. (News, 18 July 1978. neg 2061.78.21)

Familiar faces disappear (and sometimes come back again): *The Coveney sub-postmaster, Mr Harold Ding, will be retiring for the second time next week. "This time it will be for good", he said yesterday. Mr Ding, who has worked in the Post Office for 53 years first gave up the job in 1959 when his daughter, Mrs Marjory Few, succeeded him. But when she left the village to live in Cambridge Mr Ding again stepped behind the Post Office counter. "I began at the Post Office in 1917", said 76-year-old Mr Ding, who has lived in Coveney all his life. "Then, of course, I was just the village postman." He became sub-postmaster in 1942, and retired for the first time in 1959. Now a new sub-postmistress will be taking over. Mr Ding said he would be taking things more easily and there would be no more jobs, not even for the Post Office. (News, 16 October 1970. neg 18609)*

A view of the post office as it had appeared in 1921 was featured in the *News* in July 1986.

Together with a view of the main street from the same period.

The previous two photographs were part of an article which described Coveney as "A village that is fighting for its life." *On a bright summer's day, Coveney looks every inch the idyllic English village. Ducks waddle freely across the green, gardens blaze with flowers and there is a clear view of Ely Cathedral across the flat fen. But when the village school closed its doors for ever last week, it seemed like*

another nail in another rural coffin. These days there is no shop or pub in the village of just over 300 people, and only a once-a-week bus service to Ely Market. At one time the church had its own rector, now he is shared with two other villages. Mrs Rosemary Butcher remembers when there were two shops and two pubs in the village, and a doctor from Sutton held a regular surgery. The last pub went 23 years ago and the shops are gone too. Today Mrs Butcher places an order with a mobile grocery shop which comes to the village twice a week. Villagers fought long and hard to save the two-class primary school with its 27 pupils. But when the battle was lost and the last day came it was with a service of rejoicing that the life of the village school came to an end. Already villagers have formed an activities club for local youngsters to help give them a sense of belonging. (News, 25 July 1986. neg 417.86.1a)

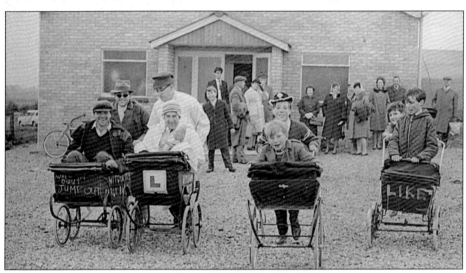

Despite the pessimism of the 1980s Coveney flourishes, though it has been some time since its streets quite saw the excitement of May 1965 after the opening of its new village hall.

Coveney village hall was officially opened by Mr Chris Kelly of Anglia TV. The hall cost £2,000 and took one year to build. Villagers spent three years raising the money. The opening celebrations included a carnival parade of 12 floats, a fancy dress competition, clay pigeon shoot and pram derby. Mr W.H. Constable, chairman of the village hall trustees, said: This is a great day for our village life. We all know each other better for our getting together to build the hall." He paid tribute to all who had worked for the project and added: "I hope the same spirit will prevail in the days that lie ahead." Mr Kelly told villagers: "Coveney now has a meeting place and a heart." Miss Linda Norman won the fancy dress competition, Hazel Day came second and Joy Freeman third. Roger Spencer of Coveney and Michael Bates of Witcham won the pram Derby. (News, 10 May 1965. neg 435/C)

Little Downham, Oxlode and Pymoor

In August 1976 villagers turned out as signs proclaiming Little Downham as the best kept village in Cambridgeshire were unveiled.

The parish council chairman, Mr Alan White said: "I'm very pleased that we came out on top but I don't know how we did it." The Fairhaven award for the best-kept village in Cambridgeshire was unveiled by Lord Fairhaven, whose uncle gave the sign about 20 years ago at the start of the county competition. He said he had visited the village before making the presentation and had been impressed by the work of councillors, voluntary helpers and individual householders. Most of the residents' gardens which he saw were, he said "immaculate and a blaze of colour – a difficult thing to achieve in present conditions. (News, 24 August 1976. neg 2516.76.18)

The unveiling of the village sign at Pymoor by Parish councillor Graham Lark caused controversy in May 1980. It was not the carved oak design depicting a dragonfly settling on a bulrush in marshland – a reference to the village name which means 'flies over a bog', nor its position in the centre of the village. The problem was the spelling of the name itself – should it perhaps have been

'Pymore' as some residents believed, and as the sign at the entrance to the village proclaimed. The question was put to the vote in January 1997 when the Parish Council declared that the name on the sign was indeed the correct one. (*News*, 29 May 1980. neg 1621.80.13)

Little Downham's Main Street, from the corner of Pond Lane, August 1981. (*News*, 17 August 1981. neg 3198.81.42a)

High Street looking towards the church, December 1989. (*News*, 1 December 1989 .neg 4502.83.9a)

LITTLE DOWNHAM, OXLODE AND PYMOOR

Work on the church bells was undertaken in 1983: *Restoration work on St Leonard's church at Little Downham has begun with workmen taking the bells out of the tower. Two men from Whitechapel Bell Foundry, London, removed the four bells – the smallest weighing five hundredweight and the largest seven-and-a-quarter hundredweight – from their mountings and gently lowered them the 30ft from the bell tower. The bells, two of which are dated 1659, the third 1702 and the other 1784, are being sent to the foundry for retuning – a job which will cost about £3,500. The rector, the Revd John Hodder explained that it represented phase one of the restoration work. Now that the bells have been taken out stonemasons will repair the crumbling tower to strengthen it before they are replaced. The whole project would cost about £10,000 to complete.* (News, 20 April 1983. neg 1507.83.9)

With improved transport far fewer people now live in isolated areas and facilities once essential to community life are now no longer needed. *A tiny wooden church in the Fens has not been used for a year because nobody lives near it. Now the Rector, Revd Martin Suter, thinks the 73-year-old building – St Owen's church, Third Drove, Little Downham – ought to be sold. St Owen's was intended as a temporary church when it was built in 1895 and used as a school until about 1963. At one time there were over 80 children attending but owing to the decline in agriculture the population moved from the droves and by 1969 there were less than a dozen children in the area. The church was closed, the majority of the furnishings, including the altar removed to a little chapel at the back of Downham church, called St Owen's chapel in its memory.* (News, 6 April 1968. neg 5302/P).

In May 1969 the church was placed on the market.

Other churches have been repaired *Restoration of woodwork at Holy Trinity church, Pymoor is expected to close the church for about a month. The woodworm has attacked most of the woodwork, including the floor, the pulpit and the altar. The Victorian church takes up half the building which also houses the village school. It has a congregation of about 30. (News, 4 August 1971. neg 5681.78)*

One essential of fenland life that needs constant attention and improvement are the pumping stations, such as that at Oxlode.

The inaugural meeting of the Littleport and Downham District Commissioners took place in 1756 at the Club Hotel, Ely. It was there yesterday that the present-day Commissioners met for a celebration luncheon before driving five miles to Oxlode for the opening of a £65,000, all electric pumping station. The station – the third, though the other two are diesel-driven – will serve about one third of the 27,000 acres administered by the Commissioners. The opening was performed by Lord de Ramsey, President of the Association of Drainage Authorities. He said Oxlode would bring a big improvement to the low-lying area in the south-east, which was beginning to suffer from poor drainage through the gradual wastage of the peat. He congratulated the Commissioners on their enterprise and foresight and

concluded by quoting lines written by Mr W.E. Doran, formerly Chief Engineer to the Great Ouse River Board:
"We formerly on wind relied,
And then the use of steam was tried.
Then came the diesel's instant power
And stayed until this present hour.
To-day another page is turned
Nor coal nor diesel oil is burned.
I close the switch and throw the mains
Comes power to empty brimming drains"
Lord de Ramsey unlocked the station doors, "closed the switch and threw the mains" and two 320 h.p. motors, capable of discharging 270 tons of water a minute throbbed into action. (News, 16 May 1962. neg Z331)

LITTLE DOWNHAM, OXLODE AND PYMOOR

Like many communities Pymoor has lost its school: head teacher, Mrs Margaret Barclay with Pymoor pupils. *Pymoor primary school closes its doors tomorrow and the school's 27 pupils will start at new schools in September. Four will start their secondary education at Littleport village college and the other 23 still in primary education will go to Little Downham primary school. Closure of the school also means closure of the parish church, built on to the school. (News, 21 July 1981. neg 2782.81.10a)*

Little Downham villagers demolished their old school: *Little Downham villagers were busy at the weekend knocking down the old infants' school in Eagles Lane in an attempt to raise between £700 and £800 from the sale of the bricks. The money will go to the Little Downham pavilion fund. About £7,000 is needed to build a new sports pavilion on the recreation ground. The school was given to the fund by the Feofees, the village charity trustees, who want the land for allotments. In return for demolishing the building, the fund is being allowed to sell the hand-made bricks and slates. A member of the fund's steering committee, Mr Michael Cornwell said the demolition would take about a month and any villager wishing to help at weekends would be most welcome. (News, 1 March 1976. neg 590.76.13)*

One of the oldest village stores in the Fens, Saberton's at Pymoor, shut in August 1986: *Putting up the closed sign for the last time was one of the area's longest serving shop assistants, Miss Vera Saberton, 72 (left). She has worked in the shop since she stepped in to help out in the 1940s. The store began trading in 1921 when Mr Hugh Saberton, her brother, opened a bicycle shop. "There was a grocery shop in the village, so my brother thought he would try bikes, but within a couple of years he started selling food as well",* she said. Her younger brother, Horace, took it over in 1937 and Miss Saberton started work behind the counter during the war while he was in the forces. Her brother died seven years ago and after that she helped her sister-in-law, Mrs Joan Saberton (right), run the shop. (News, 16 August 1986. neg 4499.86.20)

Downham Parish Council members were pleasantly surprised when nearly 100 people responded to an invitation to take a four-mile walk to mark the formal opening of a new footbridge by the Bishop of Ely. It was sponsored by the County Council Rural Management Group and the Parish Council to celebrate the completion of work to re-open a circular countryside walk in the northern part of the parish. The bridge spans a wide main drain and replaces a plank which originally crossed the drain in the days before it was widened. Parish Council chairman Alan White said: "It was heartening to see so many families enjoying an old-fashioned day out". (News 11 June 1996 neg.3801.96.19)

Haddenham and Aldreth

Dozens of villagers turned up to see the unveiling of the pictorial sign made by a team of local people. The cover was taken off by Mrs Ann Biggs, the only woman member of the team, and Mrs Brenda Hawxwell, wife of one of the craftsmen on the project. After the ceremony on the village green they each received a bouquet. The villagers opted to make the sign themselves after learning that it would cost several hundred pounds to have it made. Local craftsmen gave their time free and bills were paid from the remainder of the Silver Jubilee appeal. The sign was designed by Mr John Sheffield, and carved by Mr Dennis Hawxwell. The ironwork was donated by Mr Mike Delanoy and made up by Mr Keith Patterson. Wrights the builders supplied the bricks and Mr Tom Chapman laid them. Mr Brian Secker was responsible for the plaque and Mrs Biggs the painting. (News, 26 April 1983. neg 1568.83.2a)

Nearby another memorial needed repair in January 1983: *Damage to the war memorial, recently demolished when a car ran off the road and skidded across the green is not so bad as feared. The impact knocked the plinth off its base and sent the cross crashing to the ground. But the memorial had been built in four sections and snapped at the cement joins. Parish clerk Charles Bester said the stone work was not badly damaged apart from a piece the size of your hand that came off one corner. He said it was unlikely to be moved: "It's been there for 60 years and only been hit once." (News, 24 January 1983. neg 244.83.39)*

Mr Bester retired as parish clerk later that year at the age of 75. He had been clerk for 40 years, having initially accepted it on a temporary basis for just £26 a year. He compiled a history of the village that was distributed to every schoolchild to mark the Millennium.

One of the questions that faced the Parish Council was what to do with the old Arkenstall School: *Haddenham chemist Mr Frank Battersby is conducting a one-man propaganda campaign in support of the £20,000 proposal to convert Arkenstall School into a community centre. He has stripped his shop windows of their usual display and filled them with the plans and statements which show how the school could be converted, what the scheme will cost and how the money can be raised. The village goes to the poll on April 23 to decide whether the scheme should go ahead. (News, 14 April 1970. neg 16554/P/36a)*

The building was opened by Anglia TV announcer Peter Marshall in March 1973.

In February 1965 the *News* featured Haddenham in their 'Life in a Village' feature, when they included this view looking down the High Street. The paper reported: *Haddenham is an extremely healthy community, there are number of hale and hearty octogenarians and nonagenarians. Mr Alfred Braybrooke is 88, Mr Benjamin Jackson has lived in the village for 78 years and Mrs Ada Hudson has just celebrated her 90 birthday. (News, 26 February 1965. neg 7629B)*

The photographers returned in June 1968 for a 'Picture Parade' feature, their telephoto lens providing an unusual picture looking up the High Street with its mixture of shops and pubs. The Rose and Crown has since closed and the Three Kings too suffered a period of closure but was renovated and reopened in 2000. (*News*, 14 June 1968. neg 270/R)

They featured a number of village folk, including Mrs P.H. Berry who had worked at Croft's store in the High Street, on and off, for many years. (*News*, 21 June 1968. neg 6793/P/22)

Fifty-nine year old Herbert Gregory, Haddenham's roadman for 10 years. (News, 14 June 1968. neg 275R)

They also turned their lens on the view from the cemetery looking across to the windmill. (*News*, 21 June 1968. neg 273R)

A traditional scene for hundreds of years, a man and his scythe, is still commonplace in Haddenham. (News, 21 June 1968. neg 277R)

In their 1965 article the *News* had featured Mr John Lawrance, then 81, who had owned Haddenham windmill for more than 60 years. He came to Haddenham mill from Buckingham in 1893, at the age of 10 years. (*News*, 26 February 1965. neg 7620B)

In March 1995 mill owner Nicholas Law (right) with Gina Keene, his wife Virginia, Steven Boulton and Neil Medcalf hit the headlines: *Volunteer workers raised a celebratory glass of champagne as four*

sails were lifted into place on Haddenham's Great Mill. The mill cap went into place late last year and the arrival of the new sails marked completion of the main structure of the mill which dates from 1803. Owner Nicholas Law said: "The next stage will be a round of fund-raising and then we can get to work on the inside of the mill." There was plenty to be done to restore the mill to full working order – the old machinery is seized and rusted, millstones have to be repaired and the old brake wheel replaced. The Great Mill was one of two in Haddenham. The other has since been demolished. (News, 11 March 1995. neg 1446.95.24)

More of the village's heritage has been preserved thanks to the Delanoy family. In 1969 four-year old Craig and his brothers began collecting pieces of pottery, which were to form the basis of the Haddenham Farmland Museum, attracting large number of visitors and raising thousands of pounds for charity. They were snapped by the *News* in 1971. After the boys left home their parents, Mike and Lorna Delanoy continued to expand and display the collection until they decided to call it a day in December 1992. The Museum has now found a permanent home at Denny Abbey. (neg 5864)

While other youngsters found enjoyment on a modern version of an old-fashioned amusement at Aldreth in July 1986 (News 28th July 1986 neg.4276.86.18)

Littleport and Black Horse Drove

In April 1984 Littleport Women's Institute handed over a hand-carved pictorial sign to the village, exactly two years after starting fund-raising. The £500 sign was formally presented to the chairman of the parish council, Mr Bert Wright, by the WI President, Mrs Joan Davies. The sign, made by Mr Paul Hillard of King's Lynn, depicts village scenes on one side and the Littleport martyrs on the other. Mrs Davies said she was delighted with the way WI members had rallied round to raise the money for the sign. The fund-raising exceeded the target by about £100 after organising mini auctions, coffee evenings and a continental café at the village show. After the presentation about 90 people attended a supper in the village hall (*News*, 9 April 1984. neg 1404.84.1)

More reminders of Littleport's past are the kneelers depicting windmills, wading birds and other local themes made for St George's church by parishioners. Here the Revd Dennis Foulds inspects the first batch in November 1969. (*News*, November 1969. neg 14959/P/23)

The history of Littleport was traced back to 1770 in an exhibition at the primary school in July 1981. The display featured material from the Cambridgeshire Collection, the County Archaeologist and the County Record Office. The occasion was the publication of a *Littleport Chronicle* featuring newspaper stories about the village as reported in the *Cambridge Chronicle* newspaper between 1770 and 1899. Here Roger Rudderham shows his book to some of the people who visited the exhibition. (*News*, 9 July 1981. neg 256681

The *News* visited Littleport in May 1965 for their 'Life in a Village' feature. Amongst those photographed were village blacksmith Mr C.L. Harwood, busy at his forge. Then aged 66 he had been following his craft since the age of 13. (*News*, 28 May 1965. neg 846/C)

Mr O.T. Cross ran one of the fish and chip shops. (*News*, 28 May 1965. neg 841/C)

They also photographed Burton's shop and the traffic in High Street. *Although officially a village with a parish council, Littleport has expanded so much in recent years that its population exceeds that of many rural market towns,* the paper commented. (*News*, 22 May 1965. neg 838/C)

A quiet shopping day in Main Street, before traffic calming schemes were ever thought of. (*News*, 22 May 1965. neg 839/C)

However by December 1983 things had become somewhat busier, with yellow lines and traffic lights. In October 1982 the planners had produced their vision of the future: *A traffic management scheme, shopping centre facelift, new primary school, industry concentrated on an existing estate and a new library are among the points made in a blueprint for the future development of Littleport. It also wants British Rail to keep the railway station open and retain its inter-city services; bus services maintained and where possible improved; new houses built on a 15-acre site at Hempfield and industry to be concentrated on the Wisbech Road estate. East Cambridgeshire District Council's planning officer, Bruce Lorimer, said Littleport had its problems. The draft plan was an attempt to help it, but "In no way can it be seen as a magic overnight cure."* (*News*, 21 October 1982. neg 4502.83.6)

The Railway Station has remained open and the line has been electrified since 1969 when the News found Bert Yarwood at the Littleport signal box. He had operated the signals and crossing gates for 11 years. (*News*, 11 November 1969. neg 15076P)

Littleport becomes especially busy in Carnival week: *Littleport show got under way with a parade of carnival floats through the town. A dozen gaily decorated floats lined up at Ponts Hill before making their way through streets lined with hundreds of people. The winner of the best float competition was the Littleport Co-op staff, followed by the Busy Bees playgroup and Meadow Court residents. The guest celebrity was Lonnie Donegan, the king of skiffle.* (News, 22 July 1986. neg 464.86.24)

Thousands flocked to the 12th annual Littleport show in July 1987. The highlights included a display of low-level aerobatics, and a team from RAF Hospital Ely and another from Littleport-based Newell Packaging attempted to get in the Guinness Book of Records with a crack at the world record for potato peeling. The special guest star was Geoffrey Hayes, presenter of television's *Rainbow* show for children, pictured right with Zippy and George, who donated his appearance fee of £1,000 to the Roy

Castle Top Performers Appeal. Rosemary Hills of Soham won best working dog and best dog in show awards and Melanie Moden was named best baby. (*News*, 28 July 1987. neg 3165.87.16)

Others turned out to witness the 'Miss Littleport' competition, organised by the British Legion Band in the Constitutional Hall, in 1964 when the winner, Miss Brenda Malkin, was presented with an inscribed sash and a vanity case. The second and third prizewinners, Miss Evelyn Pettit and Miss Angela Malkin, each received a compact and lipstick. Music was provided by The Sabres band who were making their last appearance as amateurs before going off to Germany to appear at the Top Ten Club. (*News*, January 1964. neg Y4028)

But it is not all play at Littleport. Burberry's set up a factory in 1971 taking over the former Hope Brothers' factory which had been established by Thomas Peacock in 1881. When the *News* visited in September 1985 it provided work for about 150 people some of whom travelled from as far away as Downham Market each day in a company bus. They manufactured at least 14 styles of coat in a very traditional way, no computerised cutting, it was all done by hand. In May 1998 the company announced it was closing with more than 100 job losses. The factory was subsequently reopened for a brief time. This photograph shows stitching in progress in 1985; one operator made sleeves, someone else the fronts and backs and so on and it was all brought together at the end of the production line,. (*News*, 19 September 1985. neg 3524.85.9)

Nor has the factory been the only loss. In 1981 villagers mobilised to fight the proposed closure of the Village College: *Defenders of Littleport Village College walked 23 miles to protest against the threat of closure. They handed over two petitions, one signed by hundreds of parents and Littleport residents and the other by 478 of the college's pupils. Twenty pupils and staff made the long walk from Littleport to Shire Hall, Cambridge, while more than 80 pupils, staff, parents and governors arrived by bus. The pupils' petition was passed to Littleport county councillor, Denis Pye, by fourth-year organisers Joanna Richards and Susan Burton. The other petition was presented by 12-year-old Neil Murfitt, the fifth-generation descendant of a man hanged in the fen food riots of*
the last century. Watching the presentation Mr Neville Murfitt commented: "We are doing all we can to defend the village college against those who would close it down. Littleport Village College Parent Staff Association chairman, Mr John Rees, said: "The depth of felling in the village is absolutely tremendous. We were all utterly shocked that the County Council could even be considering such an idea." Councillor Pye explained: "We want the County Council to think again. We feel that once it gets to proposal stage in the committee procedure it may be too late." (*News*, 27 October 1981)

Despite the protests Secondary age pupils transferred to Ely and the Village College became a community school.

The County Primary School was in dire need of better facilities. In October 1981 the *News* reported: *Eleven of its 14 classrooms are temporary huts dotted around its tiny site. Pupils from the tots to the 10 and 11-year-olds have to run the gauntlet of Fen weather to get to their toilets, to lunch and to lessons. Games are severely limited because there is a one-mile hike to the playing fields before teachers dare hand over a ball. (News, 20 October 1981. neg 4070.81.10)*

The dining hall is so small that the 430 children eat in shifts or in their classrooms. (News, 20 October 1981. neg 4070.81.0)

More pupils had arrived from Black Horse Drove. In January 1971 the County Council recommended closure of the school and that no new staff should be appointed when headmaster T. B. James and his wife, who was an assistant teacher, retired in summer. But parents resisted the idea: if the Coronation Primary school closed the village would die they claimed. It had 27 pupils who would transfer to Littleport school which was already bursting at the seams and was inferior to their village school which was built in 1937. Parents petitioned the County Council who agreed it would not close until new buildings were ready at Littleport primary school to house the extra children. (*News*, 12 March 1971. neg 19565/P/7a)

The primary school relocated to the old Village College and when the *News* visited the new school in February 1999 they found a happy group of pupils. (*News*, 1 February 1999. neg 513.99.10)

Just as they had at the old school in May 1965 when village children at the primary school were delighted to pose for the camera. (*News*, 22 May 1965. neg 842/C)

When school is out there is time to talk about the important things in life – snapped by the *News* in 1964. (neg 998B)

Mepal

Mepal is one village that has gained a new school. It cost £18,900 to build. There was no official opening but was dedicated in September 1966 as purely a local affair for villagers. The new building catered for 60 children, and had three classrooms. In June 1990 its pupils dressed up like their ancestors from Victorian days. (*News*, 19 June 1990. neg 3889.90.31)

The new building replaced an old church-owned school, built in 1876. This was turned into the village hall, officially opened in February 1967. By June 1969 School Lane corner was a source of controversy when the Parish Council claimed it was more dangerous after the County Council had widened it. They believed drivers were now taking it too fast and there had been three accidents in five months. The County said it was not so much the car drivers they were worried about but the big heavy lorries who had difficulties getting round the corner. (*News*, 3 June 1969. neg 12762/P)

The traffic problem was solved with the opening of a new bypass in November 1985, though the route chosen was opposed by villagers who felt it would turn the village into a cul-de-sac.

The £3 million bypass for Mepal was opened officially with a blessing. After the Chairman of the County Council, Coun Keith Leonard had cut the tape, the Bishop of Huntingdon, the Rt Revd Gordon Roe, dedicated the new 2.4 kilometre single carriageway road. The main feature of the bypass is the 23-span viaduct and bridge which carries the A142 over the Old and New Bedford Rivers and washlands between. The road forms part of the Fen Link Improvement Scheme. (News, 21 November 1985. neg 4985.85.19)

Following the opening of the bypass the road through the village was closed, and the old bridge across the Old Bedford River was demolished (*News*, April 1987. neg 1531.82.17)

The lack of through traffic has not been appreciated by everybody: *A village publican claims tourism in the village is being hit because of a lack of road signs. Stuart Hammond, who has run The Three Pickerels with his wife Margaret for six years, asked for tourist signs to his pub. Cambridgeshire County Council offered to put up a sign in Mepal – but he said the only people who would see it already knew where the pub was. "There is a shortage of bed and breakfast accommodation, and we have four rooms", he said. "People passing don't see a pub from the main road – we don't get any passing trade because there are no signs on the main road and we are on a dead-end."* (*News*, 23 October 1998. neg 4857.98.6)

It has brought enhanced peace to the area around the village's church, which in December 1970 prepared to say farewell to its rector, the Revd Edward Simpson and his wife. They had played a large part in village life in the 14 years he had ministered to Mepal and Witcham. He served on the parish and village hall committees for both villages while she was joint secretary of Mepal Good Companions and Girl Guides captain. (*News*, 8 December 1970. neg 19222/P/32a)

Just outside Mepal an outdoor centre has been created from an old gravel pit: *Physical training instructor Jim McCann has a dream of turning the Mepal Outdoor Centre into a top notch activity complex open to everyone – the young, the old, the handicapped and the able-bodied. And gradually his dream is turning into reality – thanks to a bit of ingenuity, some generous cash donations and a lot of volunteer muscle. When Mr McCann of Ely left the Army's Physical Training Corps after 22 years service to run the outdoor centre his friends could not believe it. "Everyone thought I was mad", he said. "It was run down. It was crying out for investment. But when a place is down there's only one way it can go – and that's up."* Indeed the centre, part of a 30-acre former gravel pit site brought by Cambridgeshire County Council more than a decade before, had been through a traumatic time. It had been used by schools, youth and community organisations to teach the basics of sailing and canoeing. But in 1982 the county decided to close it because it was too costly to run. East Cambridgeshire District Council stepped in and it won support from Fenland, Cambridge City and South Cambridgeshire District Councils who agreed to underwrite any financial losses.

In the picture Donald Parkinson, Paul O'Neill and Malcolm Smallton rebuild one of the landing stages. (*News*, 22 March 1985. neg 1047.85.78a)

The centre experienced difficulties but by August 1995 the *News* could report: *Mepal Outdoor Centre has just reopened after a £700,000 facelift and now boasts a twin-dome roof as well as state-of-the-art leisure facilities. You can hire dinghies, windsurfs and canoes and there are children's courses on offer including multi-activity days and circus skills. As well as a new car and caravan park, leisure room and catering facilities the centre also has two rock-climbing walls. New buildings at the centre were opened by John Seaman, Chairman of East Cambridgeshire District Council.* (*News*, 8 August 1995. neg 5198.95.7)

Mepal's disused wartime airfield was revitalised in 1958 when a high fence was erected and three launching sites created for Thor missiles. They were brought into full readiness at the time of the Cuban missile crisis. The base became the centre of protest marches by the Campaign for Nuclear Disarmament in 1962: *A column of 14 cars, 12 of them carrying placards travelled through Ely to demonstrate at RAF Mepal, where ground to air rockets are housed. They were met by one police motor cycle patrolman and escorted on to an old runway opposite the main entrance to the station. After 10 minutes the column moved on, followed by seven small boys on bicycles.* (*News,* 21 April 1962. neg Z116)

The base was closed in the summer of 1963 and the site landscaped.

It has since become an industrial park, including a machinery sales ground, seen here in September 1996, and a straw burning power station has been built. (*News,* 16 September 1996. neg 5171.96.35)

Prickwillow, Queen Adelaide and Burnt Fen

These small communities have experienced considerable disruption since this view of Queen Adelaide was taken in October 1967, looking down into the village from the bridge over the river. Its peaceful appearance is deceptive. (*News*, October 1967. neg 8537/E)

By July 1979 the villagers were demanding rate cuts: *Two factories, four railway lines and the noise from a constant stream of heavy lorries has led to Queen Adelaide being described as the worst village in the country. At one end is Tilllotsons Corrugated Cases, operating up to 16 hours a day with about 200 employees. At the other end is the British Sugar Corporation's giant factory. This is the source of the villagers' main complaints. It is in full swing round the clock between October and February and is served by an almost constant stream of heavy lorries laden with beet. The villagers say the continued effects of the factories, railway lines, settling pools and lorries all help to make their village into a depressing and dying community. One villager said: "We should not have to put up with this and pay the same rates as the people in Ely. There is nowhere in Ely which is subjected to these problems. If we do not have a valid reason for a rate reduction who does? Queen Adelaide has got to be the worst place in the country. (News, 17 July 1979. neg 1833.79)*

Since then the Sugar Beet Factory has closed and been converted into a storage depot for new motor cars, with access from a new bridge further away from the village.

They have suffered the loss of many amenities: *The village of Queen Adelaide lost its only shop yesterday, after losing its school, church and pub over the past few years. The shop owners, Mrs Victoria Stevens and her son Reginald, do not have enough business to stay open. But Mrs Stevens, who is also the sub-postmistress, will keep the post office section of the shop open. The general store suffered from the decline of Adelaide as a community. "We just can't compete with the big cut-price stores. People in the village prefer to go to Ely to do their shopping rather than come here" she said. There has been a village shop in Adelaide for nearly 100 years. The Stevens have run it for 11 years. A lot of their trade was lost when the pub closed and fishermen who used to fill the village at weekends were drawn to Littleport. In June Councillor Alfred Pope told Ely Urban Council that Adelaide was dying because of building restrictions. Since 1940 34 houses had been demolished and only seven built. Adelaide is a string of houses along a road which crosses three railway lines and a river within about 200 yards. It is dominated by the British Sugar Corporation factory. (News, 6 October 1971. neg 2187/32a)*

Several pubs in the area have also closed: *The Waggon and Horses, the last remaining pub in Prickwillow, closed last night, leaving locals with no pub within four miles of the village. The brewery who own the pub, Steward and Patteson (Ely) Ltd, part of the Watney Mann group, said the pub is being closed on economic grounds because there is considerable structural failure in the building and it would be uneconomic to restore it. Prickwillow, a village with a population of more than 500, now becomes the fourth village in recent years to be left without a pub – the others being Coveney, Adelaide and Stuntney. And many villagers expressed their disapproval of the closure as they supped their final drinks in the 100-year-old pub. Mr J.T. Chapman, a regular for more than 40 years said: "The feeling of the whole village is that they deplore the closure. It could be a good house if it was altered and done up and is definitely worth the brewery spending money on it. Now they have left us with nowhere local to go with all our friends." Another regular, Mrs Howard Keel, said that there was Hiam's Sports and Social Club in the village, where they could go for a drink. "But it's really for the young people. It's far too noisy for the older people like myself, who like to go and have a game of dominoes and meet our friends." Mr Frank Bowden, licensee for the last 15 years, said there were at least six pubs within a mile or two of Prickwillow only about six years ago. He said: "I shall be sorry to leave after all this time and none of the locals like the closure. But to be fair to the brewery they must wonder if they spent any money on the pub whether they would get it back. And also they do supply the Hiam's club as well, though it's only open four nights a week and the pop dances will not really attract the older people from here". Major B.E. Dillon, a director of the brewery, said he thought the hardest hit would be the old age pensioners and those without transport. But he pointed out that there was the licensed social club in the village and public houses within reasonable distance for the many people who had cars. (News, 29 August 1968)*

Further out in the fens at Shippea Hill the Railway Tavern was under threat in July 1977 as John Gaskell discovered: *Old Dick remembers how he used to pass five pubs on his way here. But in those*

days they were all part-time landlords opening a few hours a day between their other jobs. So what happened to the area's customers? They've gone – mostly to the towns and bigger villages where they can buy a house instead of living on the farmer's land. Three years ago the Railway Tavern was one of the busiest pubs around. A lot of men worked in the station's goods yards, but they were closed down and the custom drifted away, following the farm workers. (*News,* 28 July 1977. neg 2136.77.25)

But the pub was reprieved and the few regulars could continue their domino matches for a few more years. (*News,* 28 July 1977. neg 2136.77)

Children from the surrounding fens made often long journeys to Prickwillow school – rushing home at the end of the school day in September 1977. (*News*, 15 September 1977. neg 2590.77.15)

Its proposed closure was strongly resisted: *About 100 Prickwillow villagers waving banners and singing protest songs marched on the village primary school as the latest stage in the campaign to save it from being closed. The march was organised to mark the first day back at school for the village children – who during the long summer holidays learned Cambridgeshire County Council had started the formal consultation process for closing down the school. Pupils would have to travel to schools in Ely. Protesters marched from Old Bank to the school gates led by a tractor and trailer carrying a replica of the 120-year-old school. In the playground one of the protest organisers, Mr Derek Andrews, read letters from Isle of Ely MP Mr Clement Freud and local county councillor, Mr Denis Pye. The chairman of the school governors, Canon Neil Munt, said the Parochial Church Council had unanimously passed a resolution deploring the closure plan. "We stand shoulder to shoulder with you all in our determination to stop the closure of the school", he said. The parents are unhappy about letting children of four or five years old go four miles to Ely, which would make their school day longer. One of the most determined people on the march was one of the oldest, 84-year-old Mrs Lily Norman of Kingdon Avenue, who first went to the village school when she was nine. She said firmly: "We are not going to let it close."*

The opposition was unsuccessful. (*News*, 9 September 1982. neg 3213.82.40)

Villagers were also upset in January 1967 after the *News* reported that Council house tenants in the Ely rural district might be banished to outlying villages if they fall behind in their rent.

Prickwillow, the village that doesn't want to be a "Botany Bay for Ely" called on Ely Urban Council to demand a "full and complete public apology" for what they consider a slur at a meeting attended by between 80 and 90 people. Mrs Lilian Rice, the Women's Institute president said: We have resented the implication that Prickwillow was the

place where people should go who would not pay." Mr Keith Stacey said he was fighting for the principle of not wanting the village to be slurred. The village shopkeeper, Mr Clifford Butcher, called it "a most deplorable situation brought about by an absolutely stupid suggestion." Said Mrs Frances Bourne: "This is a happy and friendly village." (News, 17 January 1967. neg: 9294/D)

Prickwillow's main street, January 1967. (News, 17 January 1967. neg 9005/D)

In March 1962 the scene had been one of activity: *Work being carried out on building a new bridge over the River Lark at Prickwillow. The old bridge is being replaced because it is situated on a double bend. When work is completed, in an estimated six months time, the bridge will form part of a straight road over the river. The new bridge is being built under the guidance of the Highways and Bridges Department of the Isle of Ely County Council.* (*News*, 2 March 1962. neg K8162)

In 1978 Prickwillow villagers called a public meeting to see if they should set up their own parish council: *Prickwillow's postmaster Mr Timothy Allen said: "We are very jealous of our identity and some of us feel we are in danger of losing it over the years. We already have a large community of young*

people so we are quite a going concern. It's got a strong community so a parish council would really be one step further." The village already has a thriving village hall committee on which the local association clubs are represented. It has a voting population of about 400. Traditionally, along with other small communities circling the city it has been incorporated within the urban area.

The meeting decided against forming a Parish Council and the Post Office subsequently closed. (*News*, 15 September 1978. neg 2633.78.10)

Prickwillow Pottery brought a new enterprise into the village, attracting large numbers of visitors: *When Margot and Derek Andrews gave up their teaching jobs to set up as potters they gave themselves two years to see if the venture would work. They made it. Not only have the two years passed but this year they celebrate the fifth anniversary of their pottery. They decided to sell their own Edwardian house and use the proceeds to set up a pottery. They looked around for inexpensive premises and found at Prickwillow some disused coal offices and sheds. Buying the premises, doing essential repairs and equipment for the pottery took most of the money they had realised on the sale of their house. At first the Andrews both worked 10 hours a day, seven days a week. A paper loss during the first year was converted into a gross profit three years later. They have relied on the help of two women who work part-time at the pottery, doing all sorts of different tasks from skilfully loading the large kiln to making cups of coffee for visitors. The visitors are something the Andrews never originally anticipated. Most of their orders come from people who have looked round the workshops. A number arrive at Prickwillow on boating holidays. Greater numbers come in groups in the evenings to look round the pottery.* (*News*, 22 May 1980. neg 1503.80.13)

They retired in September 1994.

A fen drainage museum thought to be the only one of its kind in the country opened in 1983. In January 1985 plans were announced to extend and improve the facilities in the old pump house, to include better display areas, lavatories and storage. One of the main attractions is the giant 1924 Mirrlees diesel pump, the only surviving machine of its kind still in working order. But since the museum opened a number of other attractions have been added to the ever-increasing collection of engines and artefacts. The plans were realised and the museum attracts visitors from around the world (*News*, January 1985. neg 222.85.1)

Restoration work on the church roof attracted great support: *The organisers of the sign-a-tile scheme at Prickwillow Church have had a few embarrassing moments. After inviting people to inscribe their own personal message on roof tiles as a way of raising money for restoration they ran out of tiles. Problems arose because the suppliers of the 5,000 tiles needed to re-roof the nave and porch failed to deliver them on time. Village builder, Mr John Morley, who is to carry out the work had to dash to Chatteris and grab as many as he could. The first tiles were signed by the Mayor of Ely, Coun Mrs Florence Oakey and the Bishop of Ely, the Rt Rev Peter Walker. Another was signed by Miss Lavinia Bidwell of Prickwillow, who gave £1,000 to get the scheme under way. (News, 5 October 1982. neg 3613.82.23a)*

Inside the church during a special service, January 1983: *The annual Plough Sunday service, which marks the start of the agricultural year, was held at Prickwillow Parish Church on Sunday. The traditional service is a long-established event at Prickwillow, although in many parishes, it is no longer held and, in others, it has only recently been revived. The service was conducted by the Vicar, Canon Neil Munt, and among the congregation was the Mayor of Ely, Coun Mrs Florence Oakey."* (News, 13 January 1983. neg 61.83.6a)

More recently Prickwillow has been revitalised with a new village hall and children's' play equipment: *Prickwillow youngsters are spending the summer holidays enjoying a new £12,000 play area. Slides, swings and a climbing frame, complete with safety surface, have been made available thanks to grants from East Cambridgeshire District Council and the City of Ely Council. A grand opening ceremony was held with special guests including the chairman of East Cambridgeshire District Council, Coun James Fitch and Ely mayor John Wilson. The village's previous play area was deemed unsafe and out of date. The village hall committee bought extra land next to their hall for it to be sited and applied for the grants. Janet Roberts, whose husband Paul is chairman of the committee, said: 'It is certainly very popular and the children are down there all the time.'"* (News, 13 August 1996. neg 6345.96.13)

Stretham

When the Revd Dennis Foulds was first appointed Rector of Stretham in 1955 he was told by his predecessor, the Revd John Cowgill: "Stretham may not be the most beautiful place in England but they are a great crowd." Mr Foulds, now Vicar of Littleport, revealed this secret after his former parishioners had given him a tape recorder and his wife a clock. The gifts were presented to them in the church hall by Miss S. Kitson, church councillor for 25 years and secretary for 21. (News, 5 July 1966.)

Despite Rev Cowgill's comment Stretham presents a not unattractive aspect when seen from the churchyard; its fourteen-century village cross, the Post Office – which still sells the News – is now the last of the village's shops, Joe Garner's butcher's shop is but a memory and the Chequers is a private house. (neg 6682/E)

Another was William (Bill) Lythell, the village's bobby for many years: *Going on the beat for P.C. William Lythell has for nearly 20 years meant stepping outside his own front door and making a tour of the village in which he was born and brought up. Now, just 24 years after he joined the police force as a war reservist, P.C. Lythell is retiring. He was called for duty one September morning in 1939 and only a matter of hours later, found himself in uniform, pacing the streets of Ely. Five years later he was transferred 'home' to Stretham where he had to overcome his initial reluctance at representing the law in a place where everybody was his friend. One of the few members of the Ely Constabulary who still rides a pedal cycle on duty, P.C. Lythell says he has thoroughly enjoyed his work.* (*News*, August 1963. neg Y583)

One man who knew the village better than most was the village roadman: *Stretham residents value their roadman, Mr Adna Sennitt, so much that they no longer want to share him with other nearby villages. More than three-quarters of Mr Sennitt's work – sweeping, road-patching, grass-cutting, cleaning drains – is done in Stretham. Parish councillor Mr Russell Wright said: "He does a good job. There is no doubt he helped us win the best-kept village competition."* (*News*, 28 March 1969. neg 10926/P/19a)

He became a parish councillor and was the obvious choice to plant the Jubilee Oak on the Recreation Ground in 1977.

One of Bill Lythell's roles, both as a policeman and after his retirement, was to lead the annual village Feast parade, when decorated lorries, filled with children, collect money for charity – as here in May 1972. (neg 6597P/32a)

The village school had been opened due to the enthusiasm of an earlier Rector, Revd Hugh Pigot in 1872 and served the village for over 100 years. Here in June 1968 children enjoy a break from the classrooms. Headmaster Trevor Williams was overjoyed when news came through in 1976 that a new school would be built. (*News*, 7 June 1968. neg 6656/P/20)

The new County Primary School was opened in June 1978 by the chairman of the managers, Mrs Beatrice Stevens, who unveiled a commemorative plaque just outside the front doors. Mrs Stevens, who went to school in the village, and later taught there, said the new building was in a "lovely setting", and it was something of which the village should feel "very proud." (*News*, 15 June 1978. neg 1659.78)

Cliff Knight was appointed head of Stretham school on the retirement of Trevor Williams. In 1993 it was his turn to move on: *Stretham primary school head teacher, Cliff Knight, bid an emotional farewell to pupils when he left to take up a new job in Cambridge. Each of his pupils took a flower and made up a huge bouquet on the day he left. His gifts included a radio, gold pen and picnic set. His philosophy of teaching is simple: "I believe the best gift we can give out children is confidence."* (*News*, 29 July 1993. neg 4407.93.14a)

The old parish room which had served the village since 1896 was greatly extended in October 1961. The dedication began with a service in St James' church attended by more than 200 people. Villagers then packed the new church hall where the Chief Constable of Huntingdonshire and the Isle of Ely proclaimed the building open. The alterations had cost £2,400. News photographers recorded the platform party – including a number of prominent residents. (*News*, 18 October 1961. neg K5904)

The audience in the new parish hall itself. (neg K5905)

For many years the village doctor saw his patients in the front room of a private house in High Street: *The Misses May and Cynthia Acred are the epitome of everyone's favourite maiden aunts. They have lived in their yellow-brick cottage with the purple paintwork and curtain lace all their lives – the best part of 80 years. There is hardly a family in the village which has not been grateful to the elderly sisters, for their house has been a regular calling point for the local doctor for 73 years. At first the prescriptions were delivered to the house by the village postman, then the Ortona Bus Service took over and the young girls had to go across to the Red Lion to pick up the packets each day. When their father died in 1948, they carried on the service. They have been used to patients calling at all hours for their prescriptions. Now Dr Richard Wolfendale, who has been the calling doctor for 30 years, is retiring and the Misses Acred have decided that now is the time to retire their house too.* (*News*, 9 July 1987. neg 2810.87.25a)

Like all villages Stretham has changed greatly over the last 40 years but it still retains much of its character: *A collage depicting the history of the village was unveiled at St James' church. It highlights various focal points in eleven different scenes, including the school, windmill and pumping station. Angela Fordham, who was in charge of the project, which was carried out by 13 talented villagers said: "It is a good pictorial history." It was made to commemorate the 775 anniversary of St James' and was displayed for the first time at the church's flowers and paintings exhibition.* (*News*, 18 September 1997. neg 7273.97.21)

Stuntney

The small community at Stuntney sits high on a ridge, overlooking Ely and is approached along a former causeway through the fens which has proved difficult for road engineers throughout the centuries. In 1986 came a breakthrough: *The latest road-building techniques have been used in a new £2m bypass at Stuntney. It is hoped that the special features of the new road construction will ensure it does not sink into the soft peat in the area. This was a recurring problem with the stretch of causeway*

between Stuntney village and Ely, which the 2.5 km bypass replaces. At the opening ceremony the Mayor of Ely, Mr Ron Meadows, said: "It is a wonderful achievement. The old road was all ups and downs, like a Jollity Farm". The road builders used special bitumen binders to give more flexibility and nylon reinforcements to add strength. The by-pass is part of the A142 Fen Link Road programme. (News, 19 December 1986. neg 6265.86.17)

With the opening of the bypass village streets became quieter than ever before, and eventually even the clop of heavy horses' hooves has fallen silent, when Cole Ambrose's farms finally switched to modern methods. Here in January 1965 John Reynolds and his horses make their way towards Ely in the snow. (*News*, 4 January 1965. neg 4817B)

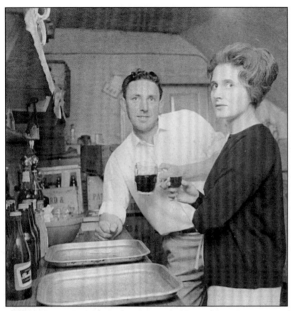

Like other small communities they have lost many of their facilities: *Stuntney – adult population about 150 and once the possessor of two public houses – has become a village without a pub. When Mr Victor McGee, licensee of the Anchor Inn, shut the doors last night, he was doing so for the last time. The tenancy has been in his family for 50 years. The owners, Steward and Patteson Ltd of Ely, have decided that it would not pay to repair a "very old property that has outlived its time." Last week a petition signed by over 60 villagers headed by the vicar, Canon John P. Pelloe and Mr David Morbey, a farm company director, urged the brewery to reconsider their decision. Yesterday* one of the directors, Major B.E. Dillon said the board had considered the petition sympathetically but could not in the present economic circumstances, change their policy. "What is happening is that more and more people, particularly the younger, go into the towns. Such money as is available is spent on modernising the larger houses in the bigger centres, such as Ely. It is sad, but there it is." (News, 28 September 1966. neg 5679D)

The village's principal landmark, the early 17th-century Stuntney Hall, said to have been once the home of Oliver Cromwell, had been falling into disrepair and permission for its partial demolition was granted in December 1976. It was photographed by W. Martin Lane in the 1950s. (neg WML 28)

Another link with the past was broken in July 1977: *Mr Jim Leonard and his wife Ruby are to give up the village post office and general stores at Stuntney after 21 years. Mr Leonard, who ran the shop and off-licence side of the business, and Mrs Leonard, the village postmistress who has lived in Stuntney all her life, opened every morning at 7 am. Now they have cut down their hours and open for two hours on a Sunday and close every day at 6 pm, an hour earlier than before. "We have loved it and we are sorry to go", said Mr Leonard. As a farewell surprise villagers gathered at Stuntney Social Club to hand over the gift of a china shire horse. (News, 28 July 1977. neg 2126.77.10)*

The village school provided a focal point for the community: *MP Clement Freud, a champion of small rural schools, did his bit for Stuntney Primary by opening its fair. Money raised will go towards equipment and outings for the 38 pupils. Headmaster Mr Charles Bell said a good profit was expected. Mr Freud, MP for the Isle of Ely, judged a children's competition for flowers in a yoghurt pot. Michelle Page won the junior section and Andrew Coombes the infants'. A new attraction at this year's fair was clay pigeon shooting and Ely publican Mr Dick Taylor, one of the governors, provided the trophy for a wellie-throwing contest. US airmen from Lakenheath gave a display of survival equipment. The children themselves organised a game on the school's computer for adults to try. (News, 2 July 1981. neg 2481.81.15)*

In November 1981 the *News* broke the story that had implications throughout the area: *Controversial plans to drastically alter the entire education system in the Ely area are set to stir up a hornets nest of protest in the Fens. Cambridgeshire County Council is looking at the possibility of*

closing five village primary schools – meaning that scores of children, some as young as five, will be forced to make a daily trek of several miles to get to school. One of those effected was Stuntney, despite protests the school closed in July 1983. (*News*, 29 July 1982. neg 2738.82.16)

But one treasure remains, the view across to Ely Cathedral, though no longer with horses in foreground. (*News*, July 1970. neg 4817B)

Sutton

Sutton church stands high over the surrounding fenland, and attracts visitors from around the world – Romany vans in July 1991 (*News*, July 1991. neg 3295.91.17)

The church was the obvious choice for the village sign, as the *News* reported in November 1984: *Sutton Women's Institute's oldest serving member unveiled the new village sign as part of the diamond jubilee celebrations of the WI in the village. Seventy-nine-year-old Mrs Ivy Blinch revealed the £500 sign to the villagers and chairman of the Parish Council Coun Philip Read, at the green opposite the village school.*

The double-sided sign, which was made by Mr Paul Hillard of King's Lynn, features a portrait of St Andrew's Church with a horse and haycart on one side, and a scene of Sutton Gault at sunset on the other. It had been originally intended to position the sign on the roundabout outside the Brook House

pub, but when the County Council said the road layout was going to be altered the alternative position opposite the school was chosen. The eight-foot high sign was set in place by employees of Darby's of Sutton, who supplied the brick base and labour free of charge. At the unveiling are (left to right), Ivy Blinch, Council chairman Philip Read and WI members Mrs Janet Townsin (secretary), Mrs Glenice Evans (president) and Mrs May Rickard. (News, 15 November 1984. neg 5420.84.5)

Other residents have campaigned for improvements: *Twenty people who live at The Row are threatening to withhold their rates until a long-awaited improvement is carried out to a 300-yard stretch of road outside their home. They are complaining about potholes and mud. Mrs Agnes Taylor said she had filled in one pothole outside her house three times. The County Council says a widening and resurfacing scheme began three years ago. They were tackling one length each year.* (News, 27 January 1967. neg 9398/D)

The view from the church tower has changed very little over the years commented the *News* in June 1967 when it visited for a 'Village Life' feature. Since then there has been significantly more development. (*News*, 30 June 1967. neg 5907/E)

They found Ellis Flinders, 80, Arkie Wayman, 68, Albert Haddock, 77 and James Rawlings, 86, chatting over the old days. (*News*, 30 June 1967. neg 5914/E)

On an earlier visit in November 1964 the *News* commented: *Cows are frequently seen being driven through Sutton's streets.* (*News*, 27 November 1964. neg 3224B)

Sutton church's unusual, tiered tower dominates the centre of the village, even on a rainy day. (News, 27 November 1964. neg 3219B)

In Sutton there is varied employment, including Brian Painter who runs the County Council library. (News, 27 November 1964. neg 3329B)

Post Office assistant Mrs H. Painter. (News, 27 November 1964. neg 3328B)

At Ibbotts' Garage there is plenty of work for Mr Jack Blinch who has worked there for 30 years, and the owner Mr M.J.A. Powell. They have the only garage in this village of nearly 1,500 people. (News, 27 November 1964. neg 3327B)

At the Sutton Primary school, the Head, Mr A.M. Williams, watches three pupils during a tape-assisted reading lesson. (News, 27 November 1964. neg 3320B)

Mr F. Higham runs the Brook House, a public house well-known by travellers. (News, 27 November 1964. neg 3326B)

The Brook House seen here in October 1983, has now closed, like so many of the village's former pubs. (*News*, 27 October 1983. neg 3939.83)

Peter Gimbert and his wife Mary turned their house into a museum. The passion started when he discovered a heap of old bottles whilst putting up a fence at the back of their garden. The house dated back to the 16th century and was once a coaching inn. Soon the old kitchen was devoted to a vast collection of old beer, spirit, ink, poison and other bottles. It spread to encompass farm implements, horse bits and drainage tools and people from around the area donated items to their collection. Peter was pictured with his collection in May 1985. (*News*, 13 May 1985. neg 1813.85.34)

The area around Sutton Gault received world-wide attention in 1967 when work began on a revolutionary hovertrain to be powered by a linear motor. A 12-mile long elevated test track was planned alongside the Old Bedford River between Sutton Gault and Earith, though only part was built.

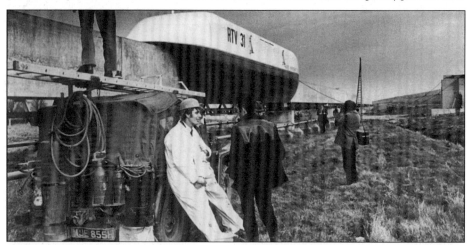

The prototype vehicle RTV31 was rolled out of its hanger at Earith in November 1971 and made its first run down the one-mile track the following month. The first series of tests were completed by April 1972 with speeds of 70 mph being recorded. But in November 1972 the Department of Trade and Industry officially said the Government were considering the future of the hovertrain. To try and give faith in RTV31 a test run was made in January 1973 when it reached 106 mph. In the face of growing discontent the Government continued to insist that the project had not been called off. But in February 1973 the Aerospace Minister, Michael Heseltine, made the announcement that the Government were unwilling to put another £4 million into it when there was no customer at the end of the line. The 150 employees were made redundant and everything closed down. The track was removed. (*News*, 16 February 1973. neg H12069.24)

But Sutton is not just a village living in the past: *Villagers will celebrate the opening of their first village hall this weekend. It has outlived the refurbished Nissen huts erected just after the Second World War in The Brook. The £375,000 hall is a dream come true for Philip Peacock, chairman of the Parish Council. "It is a valuable asset. It is all brand new with brand new furniture", he said. The hall, called The Brookland Centre, next to the primary school, was funded by East Cambridgeshire District Council, Sutton Royal British Legion and three breweries. It was built on land bought by the parish council, which will run it jointly with the Royal British Legion.* The News pictured Peter Hamence of the Royal British Legion, club secretary Don Murfitt, Ray Peacock of the Legion and Parish Council chairman Philip Peacock outside the new building. (*News,* 24 July 1997. neg 6006.97.20)

Little Thetford

Little Thetford is another place with a fine village hall: *Members of the Little Thetford Social Club toasted the official new extension when the Isle of Ely MP, Mr Clement Freud carried out the formal opening ceremony in front of about 150 guests. The club was started eight years ago, in a small room added on to the village hall, and now has more than 400 members. A local builder put up the brick shell*

and roof of the extension and then club members carried out most of the rest of the work. The club chairman, Mr Tony Badcock, said: "We still have a lot to do, and we are aiming to raise the money for new furniture. We shall probably need around £3,000." (News, 7 May 1981. neg 1671.81.33)

The Hall is the venue of a variety of events and meetings, including the Senior Citizens' club: *94-year-old Elizabeth Presnell has been made an honorary life member of the Little Thetford Senior Citizens' Club. Chairman Fred Turnbull said it was the first time such an award had been made at the club. "We are giving her the award because of her continuing active service with us", he said. Mrs Presnell now lives in sheltered accommodation in Ely, but still attends the Little Thetford Club. The award was made by John Seaman, of East Cambridgeshire District Council. (News, 5 August 1996. neg 6131.96.13)*

Older villagers recall a former resident of the unique Roundhouse: *Sixty-five year old Mr Albert Cox owner of Little Thetford General Stores does not want to leave Little Thetford when he retires from his shop business, so he plans to apply for planning permission to convert the Roundhouse. "I would like to retire as soon as possible and thought it would be rather nice to convert the old roundhouse. It used to be lived in up to about 10 years ago, but now it is becoming a bit of an eyesore." Mr Cox plans to have a living area and kitchen on the ground floor and two bedrooms and a bathroom on the upper floor with a spiral staircase joining the two. The cost of conversion is estimated at about £2,500.* (*News*, 8 July 1969. neg 13265/P/9)

The building was subsequently restored and Mr and Mrs Cox moved in in June 1971.

The village's sacrifices during the two world wars are commemorated on the war memorial which in 1981 was in need of some attention: *Little Thetford war memorial may be moved in a bid to protect it from attack by damp and fungus. The Parish Council is to appeal to village organisations to put up £12 towards the £240 needed to clean the memorial and replace lettering. Council chairman Mrs Elizabeth Veal says over the years a row of trees have kept the wind and sun off the memorial and so it has deteriorated with damp and fungus growing over it. They may perhaps move it to a better place in the cemetery. Vice chair Mrs Patricia Shaw said money had already been pledged by some organisations; the Under-Fives Club was amongst those raising funds.* (*News*, 7 May 1981. neg 1651.81.29)

Down by the river the old Fish and Duck public house used to serve passing bargees; it was put up for sale in June 1965. (*News*, 10 June 1965. neg 1587/C/25a)

It has been modernised and improved, with a new marina constructed in 1970: *The cost of the marina planned for the Fish and Duck Inn at Little Thetford will run into thousands of pounds, said the owner Mr Albert Cedar. As well as providing moorings for 60 to 70 boats, there will be a jetty almost 100 yards long, slipway, undercover accommodation for at least six boats, fuel and provisions store. Work has already started and a channel is being cut to allow river access to both sides of the proposed jetty. The marina, planned to come into operation next spring will have a depth of 4ft 6in. Mr Cedar said a car park would also be provided. And he is turning a nearby 12-acre field into a golf driving range. "This will not be a money-making object but an extra facility for people coming to the marina",* he said. (*News*, 1 October 1970. neg 18428/P/8)

In recent years Little Thetford has become bigger Thetford with the building of new houses; old and new residents come together at St George's church. *Works by artists and craftsmen go on show in an exhibition at St George's Church, Little Thetford. The Rev Malcolm Raby wants to make the church more accessible to visitors and the exhibition will be the first function since he invited the community to make more use of the building, which dates back to the 14th century. He and the Friends of the Church group want to use it more than once a week to ensure it can afford to stay open.* (*News*, 16 April 1998. neg 2825.98.29)

Wentworth

Whilst other villages struggle to maintain their school or shop, for the villagers of the small hamlet of Wentworth it has been the church that has dominated their community struggles. In November 1966 workmen were busy redecorating the inside of the church. The rector, Rev J.A.R. Lisney said the oldest members of the congregation could not remember when it was last done – it might have been as far back as 1868. (*News*, 26 November 1966. neg 7679/D)

The redecoration was celebrated at a service in February 1967 when the Bishop of Huntingdon, Rev. Robert Martineau, making his first visit to the parish, praised their work. The collection at the service was devoted, not to parochial needs, but for church reformation in Aberfan, where coal waste had overwhelmed a school and houses in 1966, leaving many dead, including 116 children. (*News*, 29 November 1966. neg 7678/D)

More restoration was needed in 1987: *Every time it rains, the congregation of a village church has to get out the buckets. Now they have started fund-raising in a race against time to repair the roof before it gets much worse. With winter approaching the parishioners of Wentworth fear that the bad weather will wreak havoc with St Peter's Church, parts of which date back to the 12th century. They are holding a fete at the village school to raise some of the £20,000 necessary to retile the roof. One of the organisers, Mrs Maureen Woodbine, said: "The roof is in desperate need of repair. If it rains we need several*

buckets to collect the water during the service." The priest in charge, the Rev Richard Mathews said the cost of the works depended on the kind of tiles chosen for the picturesque little church.

This photograph shows the priest in charge, the Rev Richard Mathews (right) discussing the leaky roof with churchwarden Fred Horstman and a local carpenter, Tom Wooton. (*News*, 24 September 1987. neg 4144.87.6a)

In 1999, the church was under threat of closure. By then the community had gained a parish council but it cost £2,400 a year to run the church and the village hall, which forms part of the church nave. A programme of events was put in hand to raise the money but village hall treasurer Ann Sinclair-Russell said it was reaching crisis point. She was pictured with Mary Macadie and Ian Howlett outside the church in June 1999. (*News*, 8 June 1999. neg 2321.99.11)

Wilburton

The seemingly unchanging face of Wilburton, seen in October 1965 when the village scored 88 points out of 100 to win the Best Kept Village competition. But they had to wait for their prize as the unveiling ceremony was delayed for a month because of the General Election and it was April 1966 before the sign was unveiled at the entrance to Carpond Lane. Wilburton were used to winning for in the previous five years they had won three times. For their first success in 1961 they received £15 with which the parish council bought an electric clock for the parish hall. (*News*, 29 April 1966. neg 5110/C)

Not even Best-Kept Villages can always be immaculate; during the gale of 16 October 1987, which caused devastation to trees throughout the area, the weathervane on the top of the church was sent leaning at a crazy angle. (*News*, 16 October 1987. neg 4504.87.4a)

Like many communities the village struggles to maintain the fabric of its church.

A £100,000 appeal is to be launched to save Wilburton's crumbling church. Seven-hundred-year-old St Peter's is in need of urgent structural repairs and renovations to windows and stonework. The appeal will be launched with an exhibition of village history and a display of the repairs which must be done. Members of the appeal committee were pictured in the church. Left to right, standing: Enid Freeman, Andrew Fogg, Philip Warren, Pauline Furness, Angela Yate and David Hughes. Seated are Susan Everitt and the Vicar, the Rev Michael Wadsworth. (*News*, 18 April 1991. neg 1960.91.15)

In August 1988 the church bells rang out as villagers celebrated winning a battle with county planners. Cambridgeshire County Council wanted to build a new settlement, Westmere, between Wilburton and Stretham. Residents of the two villages were alone in opposing the scheme and organised a campaign to stop the development which was ultimately successful. (*News*, 4 August 1988. neg 4178.88.14)

The view from the church, September 1963. (*News*, September 1963. neg Y838)

Wilburton boasts a number of old houses, one of which was being re-thatched in November 1970. (*News*, November 1970. neg 18802/P/14)

But it also boasts new properties, designed for local people: *Five new cottages provided by the Cambridgeshire Cottage Housing Society at Wilburton were officially opened by 89-year-old Beauchamp Pell, after who the development has been named. Mr Pell, who was a solicitor in his early years, sold agricultural land to enable the low-cost rented housing to be built for local people. Known as Pell Cottages, they were granted special planning permission by East*

Cambridgeshire District Council. With some funding from The Housing Corporation the society hopes to provide more accommodation for people with housing needs. Mr Pell said: "I am proud that the cottages have been named after me. It is good to help people and be in a position to put something back into the village." (News, 11 May 1993. neg 2794.93.17)

Iliffe Norfolk a local village historian who has one of the best collections of classics in the country, still enjoys browsing through the books in Wilburton's library, reported the *News* in their "Life in a village" feature in May 1964. Iliffe and Mr Pell often had long discussions about their shared love of the village's history. (*News*, 1 May 1964. neg Y7038)

Witcham

The *Ely Weekly News* visited Witcham in 1981 as part of a their 'Past and Present' series. They photographed the quiet village street. Even Prime Minister, Margaret Thatcher, knew of the village's charms, as she revealed in the House of Commons in November 1980: "I am happy that Witcham's population of 251 has a high standard of employment and very few troubles", she told local MP Clement Freud, during a debate on the proposed closure of the village school – which followed in July 1982 despite protests. (*News*, 14 November 1981. neg 1184.81)

In July 1967 the *News* reported the retirement of its best loved characters: *Witcham School was packed when the retiring headmistress Mrs Gladys Sulman was presented with a cheque on behalf of former pupils, parents and villagers. She has been headmistress for 39 years. The chairman of the school managers, Mr H.S. Papworth, presented the cheque with an autographed album of names of all those who contributed. The 48 pupils and their infant teacher, Mrs D. Duffield, presented her with a tea service and tray. (News, 22 July 1967. neg 7244/E)*

Another presentation took place in the Village Hall in August 1971, when Jackie White received the Queen's Guide Badge, the movement's highest award: *Jackie, a patrol leader with the 1st Witcham Guides, is the first guide in the villages around Sutton and Haddenham to qualify for the award. She was presented with the badge by the County Commissioner, Mrs Jean Holdaway. Others there included the Divisional Commissioner, Mrs E.E. Tyler of Ely, the District Commissioner for the Haddenham area, Mrs F. Keating of Sutton, and, of course, Jackie's mother. The District Commissioner for Ely, Mrs W. J. Papworth of Mepal, who has helped and encouraged Jackie all the way added: "It is a very much deserved award. She is an excellent leader." Jackie is a county school athlete – and she also does an evening job delivering the* News *in the village. (*News, *14 August 1971. neg 1714/5a)*

In April 1995 the village's thriving parent and toddler group celebrated its first birthday: *Founded by parents Shirley Smith, Sharon Richardson and Vivien Hayes, the group has thrived thanks to the generosity of local firms and residents. Cash came from local firms Constable Construction, The Motorist Centre in Ely, ESP, Alphaglas and the White Horse pub, as well as Witcham Parish Council and the City of Ely Council. There were toys from City Cycle Centre in Ely, and donations from local people. Mrs Hayes said: "Parents sit in a relaxed atmosphere where they can chat and have a cup of coffee while the children play. They are encouraged to take an active part in the running of the group." (*News, *27 April 1995. neg 2574.95.4)*

Civic pride took a knock in June 1968: *Witcham parish councillors switched to the role of a working party – with an eye to the Parish Council Associations Best Kept Village competition. The men trimmed the playing field hedge and the two women members tidied up the bus shelter.* Despite their efforts they achieved only 43 out of a possible 100 marks – a drop of 16 on the previous year. The clerk Mr C. Clark said: *"I don't think it gives much encouragement to the village, I thought the village looked as good as last year."* (News, 6 June 1968. neg 6808P)

The next year things seemed better: *Witcham parish council sent a letter to local roadman Frank E. Harrison thanking him for the way he keeps the village tidy. His work came in for praise at the council meeting when it was said that the roads and paths had not looked so clean and neat for years. Mr Harrison became roadman for the two villages of Witcham and Mepal 12 months ago when his lifetime job on a local farm ended through his then employer's retirement. "I am very pleased at the council's letter. It shows their appreciation",* he said. (News, 22 January 1969. neg 10261/P/2)

However their efforts paid off in 1973: *Mr Clement Freud, MP, presented the villagers with their trophy for winning the Best Kept Village competition. Mr Freud said to a crowd of 150 people before he unveiled the award: "I don't know how you go about judging the best kept village but I noticed Witcham was the only village which had taken down all the John Stevens, Barry Young and Clement Freud election posters. That has got to be one of the largest contributory reasons." One of the judges, Mr Frederick Skeels, said that Witcham had easily won the competition, and in particular its churchyard was beautifully maintained – always a good guide to the general upkeep of a village. (News, 3 September 1973. neg 9186/24a)*

For those attracted to the village, there was a special property available in May 1985 when the Jacobean Hall was advertised for sale. The house "of great character" came with seven acres of land. *For anyone looking for a quieter life on one of fenland's few hills, tucked in between the recreation ground and quaint church, with its 700-year-old tower, this has to be a bargain. (News, 18 January 1981. neg 1184.81)*

The village has an international claim to fame. The Witcham Village Hall Committee organised a pea shooting competition for the first time in July 1971. It was given world championship billing and has continued to attract competitors of all ages, as here in 1991. (*News*, 15 July 1991. neg 3810.91.13a)

Witchford

"Witchford could never be considered a pretty village – and never would be, no matter what we do to it", Graham Barber, former vice-chairman of the Parish Council and life-long resident in the village, told the *News* in October 1992. The article was accompanied by a picture of the village centre. (*News*, 13 October 1992. neg 6551.92.29)

The *News* had pictured virtually the same area in February 1969 after the Cambridgeshire Council had given approval to the widening and improvement of Main Street from Manor Road to Grunty Fen Road at a cost estimated at £15,000. (*News*, 3 February 1969. neg 3708/R)

By 1987 the traffic situation had worsened: *Angry villagers have organised a petition calling on the Government to give the go ahead to the village by-pass. They are angry because Cambridgeshire County Council first put forward plans for the by-pass five years ago – but nothing has happened since. Residents feel cheated and fobbed off. They feel they have been patient long enough and that it is just a matter of time before someone is killed or seriously injured. Some 650 pupils go to the village college and the infants school – right beside the main road – has recently been extended to cope with youngsters from outside.* (News, 20 March 1987. neg 1035.87.7)

The situation was relieved with the opening of the by-pass in December 1989 by the Chairman Cambridgeshire County Council, Coun Mrs Jane Brookes. As part of the ceremony she rode a and trap on the route. The road was the last part of the County Council's Fen Link Road s which over the past 12 years had involved by-passing 16 villages and towns on the A142, up the Fens for economic development. It was expected to carry more than 8,000 vehic 15 per cent of them heavy lorries. Just hours later two people were injured in a cras road. (News, 20 December 1989. neg 6397.89.18a)

One of the first people to use the road was Frank Allen, riding an old motor cycle. As the *News* reported in October 1992: *Frank Allen has always had a passion for motor cycles – and he continued to race them in competition until he was 70. He is chairman of the King's Lynn branch of the Vintage Motorcycle Club and has attended 58 TT Races and 12 Manx Grand Prix. Frank, now a sprightly 85 and retired from running his family's small garage in Main Street, has been a parish councillor for 35 years. The Allen family have a long and proud heritage in Witchford. Frank's grandfather arrived in the village in the 1840s and worked as a blacksmith and wheelwright. Frank converted the Smithy into a garage and engineering shop.* (*News*, 13 October 1992. neg 6449.92.33)

Although the by-pass has reduced the amount of traffic through the village, there were still protests in 1990: *Mr Sid Wales, head of the Rackham Church of England School, Witchford, is furious that Mrs Betty Challis, the school's lollipop lady, has been made redundant after more than 20 years. More than 100 of the 187 pupils, aged between four and 11, crossed the road twice a day. A petition had been handed over by villagers. The County road safety officer said she had been made redundant because of the by-pass. The flow of traffic outside the school no longer met national criteria for providing a crossing patrol, he said.* (*News*, 15 June 1990. neg 3814.90.8)

The school celebrated a special anniversary in 1994: *Pupils at Rackham School have been looking back to Victorian times to celebrate the school's 150 anniversary. Staff tried to find as many former pupils as possible who attended the school before 1945 – and around 30 attended a special tea party. Headmaster Sid Wales said: "They came across to the school and linked up with a small group of present-day pupils. They took each other on a tour of the school. There was a display of memorabilia from 1844 to the present day and some of our old pupils were absolutely stunned to find themselves on some of the photographs.* Guest of honour was Frank Allen, the oldest living former pupil. (*News*, 23 June 1994. neg 3633.94.2)

The village caters for older students too. In 1969: *Pupils at Witchford County Secondary School passed an average of two O-level exams this year, the headmaster, Mr E.A. Middleton said at the school's prize-giving day. Pupils who took their O-levels in their sixth year had an average of four passes.* (*News*, 2 December 1969. neg 15179P)

That year 30 fifth form pupils had made 142 entries for O-levels. More than 100 pupils had gained music awards during the past five years and in addition pupils had raised £400 for charity. (neg 15179P)

The *News* reviewed the school's progress in 1964: *The rebuilt Witchford Secondary Modern School which has risen like a phoenix from the ashes of the former Nissen hut classrooms is most agreeable. In 1947 representatives of the Education Committee met at Witchford Airfield, their aim being to consider the possibility of employing certain buildings to establish a secondary modern school to serve local villages. A start on the conversion of Nissen huts which once housed RAF Bomber Command personnel was made in December 1949. The school was finally opened on 9 April 1951. The first phase of the permanent buildings consisting of a hall, a small hall, a gymnasium, kitchen and administrative accommodation was included in the 1960/61 building programme. The remainder of the new buildings followed next year and the school abandoned the last of the Nissen huts during the summer term of 1963. It was due to the leadership of the school's first headmaster, the late Mr G. W. Dobson that the school established its place in the community it serves. The school is now housed in fine new buildings, which provide for the full range of secondary technical and modern accommodation. (News, 1964. neg Z4179)*

Remains of the old huts with the new building in the background. The school officially became a village college in October 1971 and has continued to expand. (neg Z4180)

The last of the old hangars on the war-time airfield were used by Anglia Agricultural Merchants as a grain store until 1973. The area has subsequently been redeveloped as the Lancaster Way Business Park. It retains a poignant reminder of its wartime days in the form of a museum dedicated to the memory of the men and women who served at RAF Witchford. Its principal exhibit is the engine of a Lancaster bomber that crashed in 1944 and lay buried for 51 years. The plane was shot down by a German fighter as it returned to Witchford Airfield. It crashed at Coveney and all seven crew were killed. Amateur war historian Barry Aldridge and a group of enthusiasts masterminded the excavation of three of the plane's engines. The engine was unveiled during a reunion visit of 100 former members of 115 Squadron who were based at Witchford during the Second World War. Here Christopher Tooth of Grovemere, inspects the engine, with, from left, Terry Strawson, Graham Austin and Barry Aldridge. (*News*, 20 May 1996. neg 3872.96.7)

Whether from the East or West, South or North, the skyline is dominated by the outline of the Ship of the Fens, Ely Cathedral. It is a view that has been unchanged for centuries and that will remain long after the people featured in this book of *Memories of Ely and the Fens* have faded into oblivion.

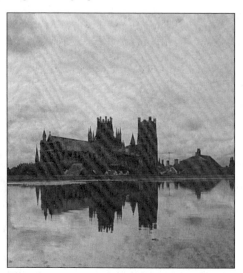

The rainwater covered roof of Tesco's store in the Market Place provided a unique view of Ely Cathedral for *News* photographer Eddie Collinson on 31 August 1993. (*News* 2 September 1993. neg 5572.93.20)

Day and night work goes on to ensure that the fenland river banks remain secure and Ely never again becomes an island surrounded by water. Despite its string of bulky barges a Great Ouse River Authority tug somehow manages to maintain the tranquility of the scene captured by Michael Manni at Dimmock's Cote in January 1976. (*News* 10 January 1976. neg 64.76.26)